THE LAST YEARS OF POLISH JEWRY

The Last Years of Polish Jewry

by Yankev Leshchinsky

Volume 1: At the Edge of the Abyss: Essays, 1927–33

Translated by Robert Brym and Eli Jany
Edited and with an Introduction by Robert Brym

https://www.openbookpublishers.com/

©2023 Translation Robert Brym and Eli Jany. ©2023 Introduction and notes Robert Brym

This work is licensed under an Attribution-NonCommercial 4.0 International (CC BY-NC 4.0). This license allows you to share, copy, distribute and transmit the text; to adapt the text for non-commercial purposes of the text providing attribution is made to the authors (but not in any way that suggests that they endorse you or your use of the work). Attribution should include the following information:

Yankev Leshchinsky, *The Last Years of Polish Jewry. Volume 1: At the Edge of the Abyss: Essays, 1927–33*. Edited by Robert Brym; translated by Robert Brym and Eli Jany. Cambridge, UK: Open Book Publishers, 2023, https://doi.org/10.11647/OBP.0341

Further details about the CC BY-NC license are available at http://creativecommons.org/licenses/by-nc/4.0/

All external links were active at the time of publication unless otherwise stated and have been archived via the Internet Archive Wayback Machine at https://archive.org/web

Digital material and resources associated with this volume are available at https://doi.org/10.11647/OBP.0341#resources

Every effort has been made to identify and contact copyright holders and any omission or error will be corrected if notification is made to the publisher.

ISBN Paperback: 978-1-80064-990-3
ISBN Hardback: 978-1-80064-991-0
ISBN Digital (PDF): 978-1-80064-992-7
ISBN Digital ebook (EPUB): 978-1-80064-993-4
ISBN Digital ebook (AZW3): 978-1-80064-994-1
ISBN Digital ebook (XML): 978-1-80064-995-8
ISBN Digital ebook (HTML): 978-1-80064-996-5
DOI: 10.11647/OBP.0341

Cover photo: *Selling old clothes in a Jewish market in interwar Warsaw* (undated), Warsaw, Poland. ©Yad Vashem Photo Archive, Jerusalem, https://photos.yadvashem.org/photo-details.html?language=en&item_id=24526&ind=123.

Cover design: Jeevanjot Kaur Nagpal

Contents

List of Tables	vii
List of Illustrations	ix
Introduction	xi
Robert Brym	
About the translation and the translators	xix

Background   xxi

1. On the Sociology of Polish Jewry	1
A. Introduction	1
B. Population density and geographical segregation	3
C. Socio-economic segregation	8
D. Political segregation	17
E. The influence of heritage	19
F. The crisis	21
2. The birth pangs of the Jewish working class	31
3. The heritage of the Jewish factory owner	45

Foreground   57

4. National Bolshevism	59
5. A flood of small promissory notes	71
6. Jews are collapsing in the streets from hunger	81
7. At night in the old market	95
8. Three-quarters of the Jewish population lack enough to live on	103
9. The destruction of Jewish economic life in Lodz	113

10. Fallen Jewish Vilna	125
11. The superfluous	135
12. Emigration tragedies	141
Index	149

List of Tables

Table 1	Polish cities with more than 20,000 Jews, 1931 census	5
Table 2	Percent Jews by selected city, 1897 and 1921	7
Table 3	Jewish and non-Jewish merchants attending the Leipzig fair, 1775–96	9
Table 4	Distribution of Jews and non-Jews in the Polish labour force, 1921, percent in parentheses	10
Table 5	Former occupations of large and middling Jewish entrepreneurs, percent in parentheses	46
Table 6	Income groups, Polish Jewry, early 1930s, in percent	110
Table 7	Percent Jews and Jewish municipal workers and officials by city	123

List of Illustrations

Fig. 1   *A sign on the shop of Torobski, an anti-Semite* (1930s), Mlawa, 12
Poland. ©Yad Vashem Photo Archive, Jerusalem.

Fig. 2   *Brzeziny. A portrait of a tailor and six members of his family,* 32
together at work (undated), Brzeziny, Poland. ©Archives of
the YIVO Institute for Jewish Research, New York.

Fig. 3   Bronisław Wilkoszewski, *Fabryka Tow. Ak. Poznańskiego* 50
(1896), Lodz, Poland. The Poznanski textile factory.
Wikimedia, https://commons.wikimedia.org/wiki/
File:Bronis%C5%82aw_Wilkoszewski_%E2%80%93_
Fabryka_Tow._Ak._Pozna%C5%84skiego.jpg

Fig 4   Untitled handwritten note (1931), Vilna, Lithuania. 74
©Archives of the YIVO Institute for Jewish Research, New
York.

Fig. 5   *A woman sitting next to a corpse in the street* (undated), Lvov, 82
Poland. ©Yad Vashem Photo Archive, Jerusalem.

Fig. 6   *A street scene, in the Baluty neighbourhood* (1930s), Lodz, 116
Poland. ©Archives of the YIVO Institute for Jewish Research,
New York.

Fig. 7   Untitled handwritten appeal (1923?), Vilna, Poland. 128
©Archives of the YIVO Institute for Jewish Research, New
York.

Fig. 8   Poster (undated), Warsaw, Poland. ©Archives of the YIVO 147
Institute for Jewish Research, New York.

Introduction

Robert Brym

Works of high sociological merit share three features. They identify social-structural forces that are largely unknown to the casual observer. They provide an historical appreciation of the origins of those forces. And they empathically portray the impact of those forces on people's everyday lives. This and a companion volume[1] qualify as works of high sociological merit, so defined. They offer the richest available sociological account of Polish Jewry in the interwar period. Moreover, they do so with the poignancy that comes from the reader knowing that this second largest but "most nationally conscious, militant, and proud part of world Jewry" (p. 1, below) was fast approaching the end of its 1,000-year history.[2]

---

1 Yankev Leshchinsky, *Erev khurbn: fun yidishn lebn in poyln, 1935–1937* [On the Eve of Destruction: On Jewish Life in Poland, 1935–1937], (Buenos Aires: Tsentral-farband fun poylishe yidn in argentina, 1951), https://www.yiddishbookcenter.org/collections/yiddish-books/spb-nybc208374/lestschinsky-jacob-erev-hurbm-fun-yidishn-lebn-in-poyln-1935-1937.

2 Some 380,000 Polish Jews survived World War II, around 11.5% of Poland's 1939 Jewish population. Most of the survivors fled to Russia. Many of them returned to Poland in the war's aftermath. However, they were often greeted with hostility, especially when they sought to reclaim property; Poles killed an estimated 1,500 Jews between the end of the war and 1947. The Communist Party sharply restricted organized Jewish life in 1949. The end of Stalinism and a brief period of liberalisation beginning in 1956 unleashed an outburst of antisemitism from below that resulted in a wave of Jewish emigration. A wing of the Communist Party initiated an anti-Jewish campaign in 1968 resulting in a second emigration wave. By 2021 only about 4,500 Jews remained in Poland. Michael Checinski, 'The Kielce Pogrom: Some Unanswered Questions ', *Soviet Jewish Affairs* (5, 1: 1975), 57–72, https://doi.org/10.1080/13501677508577206; Antony Polonsky, *The Jews in Poland and Russia: A Short History* (Oxford: Littman Library of Jewish Civilization, 2013), pp. 380–462, https://doi.org/10.3828/liverpool/9781906764395.001.0001; Paul Lendvai, *Anti-Semitism without Jews: Communist Eastern Europe* (Garden City N.Y.:

Yankev Leshchinsky, the author of this volume, was born in 1876 in Horodyshche, Ukraine—a *shtetl* (a small town with a large percentage of Jews) about 160 km (100 miles) southeast of Kiev.[3] At 18, having rejected his traditional Jewish upbringing and education, he ran away to Odessa. There he joined the followers of cultural Zionist Ahad Ha'am and studied as an "external" student, completing the eight-year Russian gymnasium program in three years. In 1901 he spent six months attending classes at the University of Bern, Switzerland, where he came under the sway of Russian socialists.

By 1903 Leshchinsky had become a leading figure in the young labour Zionist movement. For the rest of his life he vacillated between labour Zionism and left-wing Jewish diasporism, the latter of which held that Jewish life could flourish and help to achieve justice and equality outside a Jewish homeland.

Leshchinsky became head of the Berlin office of the New York Jewish daily *Forverts* (*Forward*) in 1921. It was the most widely read Yiddish newspaper in the world, with a circulation of more than 275,000 in the late 1920s and early 1930s. While chapters 2, 3, and 7 of this volume are revised from a book Leshchinsky published in Berlin in 1931,[4] most of the essays were originally written for the Yiddish press. Many of them consequently have a journalistic flavour—but they are all informed by Leshchinsky the social scientist, who, after all, was appointed head of the Economics and Statistics section of Vilna's famed Jewish Scientific Institute (YIVO) in 1925.

Leshchinsky was arrested by the German police in 1933 because of his work for the *Forverts*, but after four days in prison, pressure by the US State Department led to his release and expulsion from Germany. He continued his work for the *Forverts* in Warsaw until, in 1937, his reportage

---

Doubleday, 1971); Sergio DellaPergola, 'World Jewish Population, 2021', in *American Jewish Year Book 2021*, vol. 121, ed. by Arnold Dashefsky and Ira M. Sheskin, (Cham, Switzerland: Springer, 2022), p. 387, https://doi.org/10.1007/978-3-030-99750-2_8.

3   For brief overviews of Leshchinsky's life and work, see Gur Alroey, ' Demographers in the service of the nation: Liebmann Hersch, Jacob Lestschinsky, and the early study of Jewish migration', *Jewish History* (20, 3/4: 2006), 265–82, https://doi.org/10.1007/s10835-006-9006-3; Gennady Estraikh, 'Jacob Lestschinsky: A Yiddishist Dreamer and Social Scientist', *Science in Context* (20, 2: 2007), 215–37, https://doi.org/10.1017/S0269889707001251.

4   Yankev Leshchinsky, *Di ekonomishe lage fun yidn in poyln* [The Economic Situation of the Jews in Poland] (Berlin: 1931), https://www.yiddishbookcenter.org/collections/yiddish-books/spb-nybc210942/lestschinsky-jacob-di-ekonomishe-lage-fun-yidn-in-poyln.

led the Polish government to deny him re-entry into the country following a family vacation in Czechoslovakia. In 1938, Leshchinsky arrived in the United States, where he lived for two decades. In 1959, he immigrated to Israel, where he died in 1966.

The translations included here are based on a collection published by Leshchinsky in 1947.[5] The lead chapter was first published in 1944, but the other essays in this volume were written between 1927 and 1933, most of them in the depths of the Great Depression.

After World War I, Poland was a land of deep divisions. It faced the formidable task of integrating disconnected territories that had been tied to the Russian, Austrian, and German economies and that stood at vastly different levels of economic development. Ukrainians, Jews, Belarusians, and Germans made up one-third of Poland's population, and bitter disagreement separated the country's main political parties over the degree to which the minorities should be accommodated.

As far as Jews were concerned, 1927 was a signal year. The Polish parliament declared restrictions on Jewish enrolment in institutions of higher education unlawful. Jews were granted the right to conduct public meetings in Yiddish. A decree permitted the extension and reorganization of Jewish communal organizations. Steps were taken to support Jewish trade. Citizenship issues affecting tens of thousands of Jews were resolved. True, economic antisemitism, notably boycotts of Jewish businesses by private individuals, still took place. Institutions of higher education ignored the decree banning restrictions on Jewish enrolment. Discriminatory tsarist-era laws in former Russian areas were not abolished until 1931. And the government failed to deliver on its declared willingness to fund Jewish private schools. On the whole, however, the various Jewish factions in Poland's parliament were mollified by government policy in the 1920s. The economic front was also reasonably propitious. The Polish economy was devastated from 1914 to 1921 by World War I and the subsequent war with Soviet Russia, but GDP per capita indexed at 100 in 1913 stood at 122 in 1929.[6]

---

5 Yankev Leshchinsky, *Oyfn rand fun opgrunt: fun yidishn lebn in poyln (1927–1933)* [At the Edge of the Abyss: On Jewish Life in Poland (1927–1933)], (Buenos Aires: Tsentral-farband fun poylishe yidn in argentina, 1947), https://www.yiddishbookcenter.org/collections/yiddish-books/spb-nybc208373/lestschinsky-jacob-oyfn-rand-fun-opgrunt-fun-yidishn-lebn-in-poyln-1927-1933.

6 Polonsky, *The Jews*, pp. 222–3; Piotr Arak, 'The Economy of the Second Polish Republic Collapsed because of Dogmatic Policies', *Obserwator finansowy.pl*, 27

Toward the end of 1929, the Great Depression hit Poland with massive force. Soon, the GDP per capita index plummeted to 91 and the unemployment rate reached 25%.[7] Nonetheless, Leshchinsky initially remained quite optimistic about the prospects for the Jewish community in Poland. In his 1931 book, perhaps written mainly in 1930, Leshchinsky saw the Great Depression as a relatively short-term cyclical problem that, like all economic downturns, would end in due course. He asserted that when that happy day arrived, Jews would inevitably benefit from being well integrated into the Polish economy. They were already big players in the textile industry. Jewish petty traders and artisans were becoming proletarianized, and Leshchinsky predicted that they would be increasingly drawn into large factories as Poland extricated itself from the economic downturn.[8] Government economic policy was also problematic according to Leshchinsky. Excessive taxation permitted a bloated military budget and overinvestment in state enterprises and institutions, draining the country of private investment capital. However, bad policy could be reformed.[9]

Leshchinsky's optimism did not endure much more than another year. In 1932 he wrote:

> Over the two years since I had last visited Warsaw, the face of the Jewish quarter had changed dramatically. The people had grown paler, gloomier, shabbier, thinner, more feeble. This state of enfeeblement is undoubtedly the defining characteristic of Polish Jewry. It is feeble not only in the physical sense of the word, but also in the spiritual sense: abandoned,... without movements to captivate the masses and give them courage and faith in a better future, without great central leaders to comfort them, without central institutions to which they might direct their cry in a time of trouble (p. 84, below).

And a year later he proclaimed:

> One must look reality boldly in the eyes.... Never before was the rebuff and ejection of Jews from the surrounding non-Jewish society so strong:

February 2019, https://www.obserwatorfinansowy.pl/in-english/the-economy-of-the-second-polish-republic-collapsed-because-of-dogmatic-policies/.

7   Joseph Marcus, *Social and Political History of the Jews in Poland, 1919–1939* (Berlin: Walter de Gruyter, 1983), p. 23, https://doi.org/10.1515/9783110838688

8   The results of the 1931 Polish census, published in the late 1930s, demonstrated that, in fact, few Jewish workers were able to enter large, mechanized industries. Bina Garncarska-Kadary, 'Some Aspects of the Life of the Jewish Proletariat in Poland during the Interwar Period', *Polin* (8: 2004), 238–54.

9   Leshchinsky, *Di ekonomishe lage*.

Cultural autarky seizes ever more peoples, and it is a false hope that Jews will play the same role in the economic development of the Eastern European peoples that they played in Central and Western Europe. It is even more of a false hope that Jews will play a role in the culture of these peoples.[10]

The quickly mounting popularity of the antisemitic political right was largely responsible for the shift in Leshchinsky's outlook. Boycotts of Jewish businesses spread. A campaign to ban Jews from universities gained force. Jews were almost totally excluded from government employment. Banks strongly favoured non-Jews when it came to granting business loans. Violent acts against Jews became more numerous. The realization grew that Jews, making up just 10% of the country's population, lacked political influence let alone clout. By the time the Nazis took power in Germany in 1933, Leshchinsky among others began to doubt that there was a future for Polish Jewry in Poland and that a Polish-centred Jewish political ideology could change that state of affairs. Nobody could foresee the Holocaust, but some began to understand that the appalling conditions in which Polish Jews found themselves were the result not only of economic circumstances such as the Great Depression and misguided government economic policy but of emergent political and cultural realities that were bound to endure.

The judgment about the future of Polish Jewry that crystallized in Leshchinsky's mind in 1932–33 was not shared by the ideologically committed. Most socialists and communists persisted in their belief that proletarian revolution would rescue Polish Jewry. The socialist-diasporist Bund grew throughout the 1930s. The Zionist movement, too, recruited new members. Emigration to Palestine rose sharply from 1933 to 1936 when Britain relaxed its restrictions on Jewish immigration. Numerically even more significant were the many Jews who wavered little in their certainty that *der oybershte firt di velt* (the One above directs the world) and that adherence to Jewish law would ensure God's beneficence. Leshchinsky was well aware of their enduring influence:

---

10 Yankev Leshchinsky, 'Ofener un erlikher' [Blunter and More Honest], *Literarishe bleter: ilustrirte vokhnshrift far literatur teater un kunst* [Literary Pages: Illustrated Weekly for Literature, Theatre, and Art], 18 August 1933, 525, https://www.nli.org.il/en/newspapers/?a=d&d=ltb19330818-01.1.1&e=-------en-20--1--img-txIN%7ctxTI--------------1.

"The orthodox, religious Jews control the communities....And the dancing and fervent singing in small Hasidic houses of prayer during the Sabbath evening meal resound and overpower the songs and shouts of all national and socialist groups and circles" (pp. 136, below).

However, for Leshchinsky and a growing number of Polish Jews, the modern isms that offered them control over their destiny seemed increasingly out of touch with reality. The ascent in Europe of what Kenneth B. Moss evocatively calls extrusionary nationalism caused some independent Jewish thinkers and a growing number of ordinary Jews to reassess whether the glorious futures they had been promised still made sense.[11] They began examining the facts and pondering which courses of action, if any, were still open to their people. Moss shows that only one new ism emerged from this painful exercise: a growing realism. Realism did not produce a new mobilizing program for collective liberation. It did not anticipate the Holocaust. It was simply an attempt to look reality squarely in the eyes and recognize the limitations of old answers to the Jewish question.

True, between the world wars several hundred thousand Polish Jews escaped to the United States, Palestine, Argentina, Canada, and a few other countries. However, one must recall that the number of Jewish emigrants from Poland numbered at most one-half the community's natural increase over those years, so escape could hardly be a solution to Poland's Jewish question. This was especially the case once the Great Depression halted nearly all Jewish immigration to the West. Moreover, it was doubtful whether those who migrated to the liberal assimilative West would be able to reconstitute the conditions that made Polish Jewry the world's most socially cohesive and culturally creative Jewish community. As Moss shows, a growing number of those who managed to leave for Palestine did so on pragmatic grounds, viewing their decision more as an opportunistic escape for themselves and their family members than a reliable collective solution to the Jewish question.

This, then, was the atmosphere in which Yankev Leshchinsky wrote most of the essays in the present collection. When he composed the lead essay of this volume in 1944 the dimensions of the Holocaust were clear,

---

11   Kenneth B. Moss, *An Unchosen People: Jewish Political Reckoning in Interwar Poland* (Cambridge MA: Harvard University Press, 2021), https://doi.org/10.4159/9780674269989

and he was even more certain of the fate of Polish Jewry. He wrote in the past tense because, "regardless of the number of Jews who will remain alive in Poland, the old spirit of Polish Jewry has unquestionably been annihilated. All roots of the centuries-long national traditions have been so completely ripped out and all vestiges of them have been so utterly washed away that it is difficult to believe in a rapid revival of Jewish national life in Poland" (p. 2, below).

About the translation and the translators

We have for the most part followed the YIVO standard for Yiddish transliteration. Exceptions are Yiddish words that have conventional English spellings. We have also rendered "Leshchinsky" phonetically rather than using the conventional "Lestschinsky" because many English-only readers might find the latter unpronounceable. In previous publications we rendered Leshchinsky's first name as "Yakov" (a phonetic version of the Hebrew) because Leshchinsky lived his last years in Israel. However, Kenneth Moss has convinced us that, because Leshchinsky wrote the present volume in Yiddish, it would be more appropriate to transliterate his first name as Yankev. For this and Ken's other sage advice, we are most grateful.

All text {in braces} is the translators'. We added tables on pp. 5 and 7 and all images.

Robert Brym, FRSC, is Professor of Sociology and an Associate of the Centre for Jewish Studies at the University of Toronto. His latest work is Robert Brym and Randal Schnoor, eds, *The Ever-Dying People? Canada's Jews in Comparative Perspective* (Toronto: University of Toronto Press, 2023). For downloads of his published work, visit https://utoronto.academia.edu/RobertBrym.

Eli Jany is a PhD student in the Department of Germanic Languages and Literatures and the Centre for Jewish Studies at the University of Toronto. He has translated poems by Sarah Reisen (*In geveb*, 12 May 2020, https://ingeveb.org/texts-and-translations/three-poems-reisen) and, with Robert Brym, co-translated Yankev Leshchinsky, "Jewish Economic life in Yiddish Literature: Yitskhok Ber Levinzon and Yisroel Aksenfeld," *East European Jewish Affairs* (53, 1: 2023).

BACKGROUND

1. On the Sociology of Polish Jewry

A. Introduction

After World War I, Polish Jews played the leading role in world Jewry. Russian Jewry became isolated from the mainstream of our national and social life. American Jewry did not yet manage to crystallize itself nationally and culturally to a degree that would allow it to play the role that its size and favourable political situation might justify. The three million Jews of the revived Polish state thus remained the most important centre of our dispersed people.[1]

However, if one contemplates the issue more deeply, it immediately becomes apparent that it is not only these coincidental circumstances that caused Polish Jewry to play the leading role in world Jewry. There were many more important reasons that gave Polish Jewry the moral right to claim spiritual and political predominance, notably its treasury of national creative energy, which enriched the life of Jews in all corners of the world, including the land of Israel, and that provided the content and sap for all our national-political and spiritual-cultural movements. Polish Jewry suffered least from the whole assimilationist epoch and asserted itself as the most nationally conscious, militant, and proud part of world Jewry.

What are the factors that led the assimilationist catastrophe to be weakest and the national legacy to be the most influential among Polish Jews? What factors enabled the national legacy to be richer, more conservative and more creative in Poland than elsewhere?

We use the past tense because, regardless of the number of Jews who will remain alive in Poland, the old spirit of Polish Jewry has

---

1 {Throughout, footnotes in braces have been added by Robert Brym. In 1933, about 2.8 million Jews lived in the Soviet Union and 4.5 million in the United States.}

unquestionably been annihilated. All roots of the centuries-long national traditions have been so completely ripped out and all vestiges of them have been so utterly washed away that it is difficult to believe in a rapid revival of Jewish national life in Poland. People who have lived through three, four, five and often more expulsions; who have lived through three, four, five and often more transformations; who have seen with their own eyes the murder of children and parents, brothers and sisters, and have personally encountered the Angel of Death ten times a day—these remnants of Polish Jewry were physically unable to rescue the previously mentioned treasury of national creative energy from the catastrophe, especially because their number is so small.

Unfortunately, the time has therefore arrived to make sense of the historical factors that created and sustained the extraordinarily rich national energy of Polish Jewry.

§

Just 170 years ago, Polish Jewry constituted almost the entirety of world Jewry, not taking account of Sephardic and Arabic Jews, who then played a minor role in the life of the Jewish people as a national unit. On the eve of the first partition of Poland in 1772, 70% of world Jewry and more than 80% of Ashkenazi Jews—the main if not the only bearers of the Jewish people's national continuity—lived in Poland. All the large and small Jewish settlements that grew up in the past 150 years in Europe and in all corners of the world are biological and cultural branches of the Polish-Jewish tree, the only tree in the diaspora that managed to be suckled by one and the same ground for a long and uninterrupted period of nearly a thousand years.

Continuity and rootedness, deep traditionalism, effective inertia, healthy religious and national conservatism, an especially vital national instinct and an especially outspoken, almost conspicuous national pride, an admirable sense of national responsibility, and a maximal national discipline in comparison with all other diaspora communities—all these characteristics of Polish Jewry were to a great extent an organic result of their long and uninterrupted life in one and the same territory, under one and the same sky, beside one and the same Vistula.

Only in this way can one explain why Polish Jews are so spiritually bound to Poland, its landscape and folk culture. Their destiny is not just economically and politically linked with the fate of the Polish people. It is difficult to find among Jewish writers from other countries the romanticism regarding the landscape and the enchantment with rivers that one finds in Sholem Asch and many other Polish-Jewish writers. The Polish sky, the Polish forest, the Polish field, the Vistula's waves—all this charmed and captivated not only the refined souls of writers but all of Polish Jewry and thus endowed this branch of our people with a special grace.

However, this physical-environmental factor did not exert an assimilative influence in the national sense. It influenced the national character of Polish Jewry, imparting lines and wrinkles similar to those of the Polish people—but not more. Other factors outweighed it, factors that helped to influence the crystallization and consolidation of Polish Jewry as a separate national group and that led to the more intensive development of national unity and feeling of responsibility on the part of this branch of the Jewish people.

B. Population density and geographical segregation

The most influential factors were the simple number and density of the Polish Jewish population. In no other part of the world (aside from the small and unimportant settlement in Carpathia[2]) did the Jews make up such a high percentage of the population or form such a dense, concentrated community, the members of which embraced each other and, of their own volition, ghettoized themselves from the surrounding population.

In large parts of Poland, Jews always lived near a heterogeneous mix of nationalities, a conglomeration of two and often three peoples: in the western region, Poles and Germans; in eastern Galicia, Ukrainians, Poles and Germans; in the eastern region, Lithuanians, White Russians, Poles and slivers of Russians. The battle of languages and cultures among these surrounding peoples must have weakened the assimilative power of each on the Jewish population. The unceasing and growing fight of the most backward national groups for their national existence, language, and culture despite their poverty and primitiveness must have

---

2 {Southwestern Ukraine.}

awoken in the Jewish masses the appetite to defend their own language and culture and not give way to the stronger and richer culture of the dominant Polish group.

A minority in the country, Jews had long comprised a plurality and often a majority in most Polish cities and towns, especially in the peripheral territories of Ukraine and White Russia, where, on the eve of the war,[3] they remained a majority in many cities and towns, and the Yiddish language dominated. This circumstance was often transformed into complete national separation because in the main streets and markets Jews often made up 100% of the population. The non-Jewish population lived almost completely on the periphery of cities and towns, that is, in agricultural areas. They visited the Jewish streets and the Jewish market only for business, to sell their produce and buy various things. They lived completely apart. They served God separately, sent their children to different schools (if non-Jews sent their children to school at all), celebrated different holidays on different days and read different books (if they read books at all). Understandably, there could be no talk of biological proximity; converts were spit out of the Jewish community.

Segregation was typical not only in small towns but also in middle-size cities. And the picture is not of a distant past; until 1920, it is accurate for all areas of former Tsarist Russia, where there was still no compulsory public education. For Galicia, the picture is a little less stark—there was a high level of segregation but at least members of different national groups studied together in public school. Yet, although in Catholic Galicia the Jewish population assimilated linguistically much more than in the areas of Tsarist Russia, Jewish religious conservatism was considerably stronger than in Russia.

In the last few decades, segregation in the large cities was not so pronounced and influential. However, even there, entire sections of cities were composed of 80% or even 90% Jews. Most of the Jewish population of large cities lived in completely Jewish quarters. Only a minority, usually consisting of richer and more highly educated Jews, were scattered among non-Jews. In the large city, the Jew certainly took pleasure in Polish theatre, the Polish press, and Polish culture in general, but the density of the Jewish masses created the basis for

---

3   {Throughout, when Leshchinsky refers to "the war," he means what we now call World War I.}

their own newspapers, theatres and other cultural institutions. For the great majority of big-city Jews, Polish culture was a sort of luxury good. Modern Jewish culture was—or was becoming—their cultural bread and butter.

Table 1 Polish cities with more than 20,000 Jews, 1931 census

City	Total population	Jewish population	Percent Jews
Warsaw	1,171,898	352,659	30.1
Lodz	604,629	202,497	33.5
Lvov	312,231	99,595	31.9
Cracow	219,286	56,515	25.8
Vilna	195,071	55,006	28.2
Bialystok	91,335	43,150	47.2
Lublin	112,285	38,937	34.7
Czestochowa	117,179	25,588	21.8
Sosnowiec	108,959	20,805	19.1
Subtotal	2,932,873	894,752	30.5
Rest of Poland	28,982,906	2,219,181	7.7
Total	31,915,779	3,113,933	9.8

Source: Głównego Urzędu Statystycznego [Central Statistical Office]. *Drugi Powszechny Spis Ludnosci* [Second Population Census] (Warsaw: 1938).

Residential segregation is not specific to Polish Jews. We find it among Jews in the whole world and among other peoples too. However, nowhere else did it assume such proportions and have such an uninterrupted history. Nor did it elsewhere have such a broad, isolated economic basis, which not only strengthened and intensified the physical separation but rendered it richer and more fruitful.

The extent and duration of population concentration coinciding with socio-economic isolation played an enormous role in consolidating and cementing the Jewish minority as a national unit. These factors created a more or less healthy basis for maintaining the Jewish religion and other national life forms and transforming ancient religious cultural values into modern national cultural creations. Not only did Yiddish stubbornly persist among the great majority of the Jewish population. It also demonstrated a relatively high level of creativity and resistance to the flood of surrounding assimilative forces and a comparatively robust capacity to develop in modern circumstances and compete with the dominant political and cultural language of the majority. In no other place in Eastern Europe where, not long ago, Yiddish dominated as much as in Poland—not in Hungary, Romania, Slovakia or Carpathia—did it engage in such a stubborn struggle for existence, and nowhere else did it manifest such distinct and clear potential for organic growth as a modern cultural instrument of the broad Jewish masses.

One can say the same about the Hebrew language and Hebrew culture. In all the previously mentioned lands there were also many *cheders* and *yeshivas*[4] where Torah and Talmud was taught, but only in Poland did the ancient Hebrew culture grow organically into Modern Hebrew culture.

Let us present some figures to illustrate the spatial segregation of Polish Jews from the surrounding Polish majority.

In 1857, of 181 urban settlements in former Congress Poland,[5] 88 (48.6%) had a Jewish majority. One hundred and twenty (66.2%) were more than 40% Jewish.[6] We will see that, because Jewish storekeepers and craft workers made up 90 to 100% of this urban population, and because the Christian population was then still employed in agriculture or in jobs in which Jews were not involved, such as heavy construction, unskilled work and so on, nearly the entire population of small and middle-size urban centres was Jewish.

In 1897, of 110 urban settlements in Congress Poland, 57 (51.8%) had a Jewish majority and 81 (73.6%) were more than 40% Jewish. The number of urban settlements with a high percentage of Jews became much smaller in the twentieth century but in Congress Poland in 1921, 99 of 196 urban settlements (50.5%) were more than 40% Jewish.[7]

In Galicia in 1880, of 125 urban settlements, 55 (44%) were more than 50% Jewish and 82 (65.6%) were more than 40% Jewish. And in Galicia,

---

4 {The *cheder* was a religious primary school. The *yeshiva* "trained young men to study formative texts and traditions, especially the Babylonian Talmud, the commentaries on it, and the legal decisions that depended on it" ("Yeshiva." *The YIVO Encyclopedia of Jews in Eastern Europe* (2010), https://yivoencyclopedia.org/article.aspx/Yeshiva/The_Yeshiva_before_1800.}

5 {Congress Poland was established in 1815 as a putatively sovereign state but it was under Russian tutelage. It consisted of the eastern part of today's Poland along with southwestern Lithuania and part of the Grodno province of Belarus. In 1831 it effectively became part of Russia.}

6 Bohdan Wasiutyński, *Ludność żydowska w Polsce w wiekach XIX i XX* [The Jewish Population of Poland in the 19th and 20th Centuries] (Warsaw: 1930).

7 Ibid.

where Ukrainians also lived in the cities, Jews were even more often a national plurality. Of the same 125 urban settlements in 1921, 57 (45.6%) were more than 40% Jewish.[8]

In the White Russia region, the percentage of Jews in urban settlements was even larger. According to the 1897 Russian census, the urban population of Grodno province was 57.7% Jewish and the urban population of Vilna province was 43.0% Jewish. In Minsk province, which was almost completely absorbed by Poland after World War I, Jews formed 58.8% of the urban population.[9] Following are data for individual cities in this region:

Table 2 Percent Jews by selected city, 1897 and 1921

City	Percent Jews, 1897	Percent Jews, 1921
Brest	75.4	53.1
Pinsk	74.2	74.7
Bialystok	63.5	51.6
Grodno	59.5	53.9
Vilna	45.4	36.1

Except for Vilna, the percentage of Jews in the five biggest cities of the White Russian region was very high at the end of the nineteenth century, around three-quarters in two cities. In the smaller cities of this region, the percentage of Jews was even higher because little industry existed there; industry attracted non-Jewish workers in the big cities. One must also remember that the non-Jewish populations of these cities was composed of three peoples—four in Vilna (Poles, Russians, Lithuanians and White Russians).

Even in 1931, when the cities were naturally and by design flooded by a great mass of non-Jews, there were still many cities where Jews constituted a plurality or a majority of residents. Of 192 counties {powiats} in 13 provinces {voivodeships} that had a dense Jewish

---

8   Yankev Leshchinsky, *Dos yidishe folk in tsifern* [The Jewish People in Numbers] (Berlin: 1922), https://www.yiddishbookcenter.org/collections/yiddish-books/spb-nybc210949/lestschinsky-jacob-dos-idishe-folk-in-tsifern.

9   Yankev Leshchinsky, *Yidn in der shtotisher bafelkerung fun umophengikn poyln* [Jews in the Urban Population of Independent Poland], 12, 27 and 34.

population (Warsaw, Lodz, Kielce, Lublin, Cracow, Bialystok, Vilna, Novogrodek, Poleskie, Lemberg,[10] Stanislav, Tarnopol and Volhynia), Jews formed an absolute majority in 28 and a plurality in 23. In 53 counties (27.6% of the total), Jews constituted most of the urban population. In 9 of 11 counties in Volhynia province, Jews formed a majority of the urban population, and in the province as a whole, they constituted 55.6% of the urban population.[11]

C. Socio-economic segregation

The spatial separation of Polish Jews from the surrounding non-Jewish population was consolidated by their socio-economic distinctiveness. Until the Polish middle class arose in the second half of the nineteenth century, Jews formed a unique socio-economic organism. For centuries, they constituted such a large proportion of the merchant class that one could be fully justified in thinking that all merchants were Jews. Because of this, it was often asserted that all Jews were merchants. That was never the case, least of all in the nineteenth century, but this error was natural because, even 20 or 30 years ago, Jews in large parts of Poland made up 90% or more of all merchants.

For decades, even where non-Jewish merchants were emerging, almost all of them entered only one branch; they became owners of food stores. Only after World War I did they begin entering the main branches of mercantile activity, previously leaving textiles, haberdashery and leather and hardware sales in Jewish hands. Foreign trade was almost completely Jewish-controlled. Only very recently, when the Polish government began to regulate and plan economic life in general and the export-import trade in particular, at least to a greater degree than internal trade, did the non-Jewish (mainly Polish) exporter and importer emerge.

Let us illustrate this phenomenon with some figures, not exhaustively but just to sketch some general patterns.

---

10 {Lemberg when controlled by the Austro-Hungarian Empire, Lwów when controlled by Poland, Lviv when controlled by Ukraine, and Lvov when controlled by Russia, was called Lemberik by many Jews.}
11 Ibid.

The number of merchants from Poland who attended the Leipzig fair[12] was as follows:[13]

Table 3 Jewish and non-Jewish merchants attending the Leipzig fair, 1775–96

Year	Total merchants from Poland	Jewish merchants from Poland	Jews as percent of total
1775	481	413	86.0
1790	678	611	90.0
1796	851	791	93.1

Because visitors to the Leipzig fair used to buy textile-haberdashery and metal goods, it is doubtless the case that the percentage of Jewish attendees corresponded to the percentage of Jewish wholesalers of these items in Poland.

Of 1,441 wholesalers in all of Galicia between 1820 and 1827, Jews numbered 1,172 (81.3%). In eastern Galicia alone, Jews were 86.3% of all wholesalers. There were 2,015 shopkeepers and stall owners in all of Galicia in this period, 1,824 of them (90.5%) Jews.

Here are some figures concerning craft workers. One hundred and fifty-one of the 153 glaziers in Galicia (98.5%) were Jews, as were 1,358 of the 1,441 tailors (94.3%), 103 of 127 coppersmiths (81.1%), 42 of 57 dyers (73.7%) and 511 of 733 hat makers (70.0%).[14]

A century later, in 1921, Jews constituted 90.8% of all independent merchants in eastern Galicia and 76.5% in western Galicia. In credit and insurance, the respective figures were 90.1% and 78.8%.[15]

---

12 {In the eighteenth century, the tri-annual Leipzig Trade Fair became the German centre for trade in English, Russian and Polish goods.}

13 R. Markgraf, *Zur Geschichte der Juden auf den Messen in Leipzig von 1664–1839* [On the History of the Jews at the Leipzig Trade Fair from 1664–1839] (Bishofswerda: 1894), 21–34.

14 Michael Stoeger, *Darstellung der gesetzlichen Verfassung der galizischen Judenschaft* [A Description of the Legal Constitution of Galician Jewry] (Lwów: 1833), 200–76.

15 Yankev Leshchinsky, "Profesioneler bashtand fun yidn in eyrope" [The occupational composition of Jews in Europe"], *Shriftn far ekonomik un statistik* [*Writings on Economics and Statistics*] (Berlin: 1928), 197.

In 1852, Jews made up 96.1% of merchants in the province of Grodno and 88.2% in the province of Minsk.[16] In 1921, the percentages for independent merchants were approximately the same.

Table 4 Distribution of Jews and non-Jews in the Polish labour force, 1921, percent in parentheses

	Non-Jews	Jews
Agriculture	10,197,351 (80.7)	90,102 (9.8)
Industry & crafts	968,920 (7.7)	297,447 (32.2)
Trade & finance	194,136 (1.5)	324,612 (35.1)
Transportation	219,052 (1.7)	24,808 (2.7)
Civil service, professions	286,025 (2.3)	40,356 (4.4)
Other	768.232 (6.1)	146,703 (15.8)
Total	12,615,716 (100.0)	924,028 (100.0)

Source: Yakov Leshchinsky, "The development of the Jewish people over the last 100 years," Robert Brym, trans., *East European Jewish Affairs* (50, 1–2: 2020), 160–242 at 202, https://doi.org/10.1080/13501674.2020.1793279.

Even in 1938, after the spontaneous growth of a merchant class in Poland and a decade of the government artificially planting Polish merchants in many districts, there were still entire branches of trade that were mainly in the hands of Jews. Of 6,900 grain merchants, 6,214 (90.0%) were Jews. Of 75,551 clothing merchants, 66,024 (87.4%) were Jews.[17] These figures concern all of Poland. Considering separate districts, one finds that in the western provinces (Posen, Pomerania, Silesia), Jews made up an insignificant percentage of merchants, but they made up 100% of those employed in many branches of trade in eastern Galicia and the White Russian provinces. Also in Congress Poland, until recently, there were tens if not hundreds of places where Jews comprised more than 90% of all merchants, especially in certain branches such as the sale of textiles, haberdashery, and other articles.

Aggregated census data, especially for the entire country, obscure the actual situation. To obtain an accurate picture, one must consider individual provinces and individual social groups. Thus, according to

---

16 Dr Ignacy Szyper, *Dzieje handlu żydowskiego na ziemiach polskich* [*The History of Jewish Commerce in Poland*] (Warszawa: 1937), 414.
17 *Wiadomomości Statystyczne* [*Statistical Notices*], 1939, 5/VI.

the 1921 census, Jews made up 63.5% of those involved in trade in all of Poland. But in the province of Bialystok, the figure was 80.0% and in Pomerania, 5.0%. In the province of Volhynia, the figure was 88.1% and in Posen, 6.0%. One must also consider the participation of different social groups. Here we are reminded that in 1921, Jews made up more than 63% of people involved in trade, but 76.5% of independent operators. The Christian salesclerk working in a Jewish store exerted only a minor influence on the character of the business, and if in a given city 90% or more of merchants were Jews, they very easily could have closed up shop on the Sabbath without having any fear of competition.

Forming nearly the entire merchant class in the country, the Jew naturally must have had some relations with the surrounding population, but these ties had a purely external, business-like character. They did not lead to any intimacy with the surrounding language, which the Jew had to know and did in fact know. Buying and selling took place between two separate population groups that lived in separate cultural spheres, irrespective of the fact that they resided so close to one another and were parts of one economic organism and one body politic.

This situation can be explained not just by the religious difference between the two groups, which remained strong for centuries, but also by the fact that buying and selling took place with an almost completely rural peasant population, with a primitive and backward mass to which one did not need to adapt culturally or even linguistically. It did not matter whether one spoke Polish, Ukrainian or Lithuanian—the two parties understood one another in buying and selling. Business—big business—also took place with rich aristocrats, but these landowners viewed the Jewish merchant from such a lofty perch that it did not occur to them to demand from the merchant better Polish or closer cultural proximity. The Jew, the main buyer from and seller to peasants and aristocrats until almost the end of the nineteenth century, did not need to adapt linguistically or culturally.

Craftwork, the other main economic branch, occupied a large place in Jewish life and kept on expanding over the past 50 years. Overall, the concentration of Jews in crafts was neither as dense nor as isolating as was the case in trade. However, among urban tailors, shoemakers, carpenters, furriers and cap makers, Jews formed a large majority. These crafts accounted for 80% to 90% of all Jewish crafts workers, so they, too, laid the foundation for a segregated social environment.

Only in the last 50 years and especially the last 20 years in independent Poland did the number of Polish storekeepers and craft workers start to increase rapidly, especially in the big cities and ethnically Polish areas. The exclusivity of Jews in entire branches of economic life began to disappear. But more about this revolution in Jewish life later. Now we will discuss the increase in the number of storekeepers and craft workers among Poles; among Ukrainians and especially White Russians the urban middle class was still in diapers. And in the Ukrainian and White Russian areas of Poland, the urban Jew had much more contact with the Pole than with the Ukrainian or White Russian.

In middle-size and especially large cities, where a chauvinistic Polish intelligentsia and a still more chauvinistic stratum of Polish state bureaucrats formed, many Polish-owned stores opened in the last few years, and Poles were increasingly attracted to crafts. Polish workers' quarters in the big cities became residences for the growing number of Polish storekeepers and craft workers. For the most part, Polish storeowners and craft workers settled in new areas of the city or at least in areas devoid of Jews. Only rarely did a Christian open a store in a Jewish part of town. It was also rare for a Jew to open a store in a purely Polish neighbourhood, not because he could not compete against the Poles but because he was not allowed in due to restrictions

Fig. 1 *A sign on the shop of Torobski, an anti-Semite* (1930s), Mlawa, Poland. ©Yad Vashem Photo Archive, Jerusalem. The inscription on the left advises against buying from Jews, with an accompanying illustration illustrating their appropriate treatment https://photos.yadvashem.org/photo-details.html?language=en&item_id=8955&ind=1

of a physical rather than legal nature. The boycott was the least violent method of struggle against the Jew. The less proficient and younger Polish storekeeper defended himself against the Jewish storekeeper by physical means. He also had the support of the government, which offered credit at a reduced interest rate and lower taxes as well as other discounts and privileges.

However, we are interested here not in the struggle of the Polish storekeeper against his more capable and nimbler Jewish counterpart but in the fact that in the large cities and most of the middle-size cities there again formed a Jewish ghetto, a part of the city where Jewish businesses were concentrated. That was the case in Warsaw's Nalewki district and in similar areas of Lodz, Bialystok, Vilna and many other cities. Thus, in the larger cities, most of the Jewish population was segregated from the non-Jewish population. Moreover, the Jewish part of the city made its living not mainly from the local city population but from producing and distributing goods for the entire country and from exporting and importing goods not in proportion to the needs of the city but in proportion to the needs of the country. In contrast, the newly formed Polish city districts made a living almost completely from nearby customers.

There was in most of the big cities a "bridge" between the two national "ghettos." The bridge consisted of the central streets between the two national districts. In a completely natural way, Jews from one side and Poles from the other spread into the central streets between the ghettos. In these bridging streets, the national composition of storekeepers, craft workers and all other occupations such as druggists, restaurateurs and so on, was mixed. Here, competition was open and the protagonists about equally matched if we ignore the privileges that the government granted the Polish side and the pickets outside the Jewish stores that openly and legally called for their boycott.

Thus, during the last few decades, a part of the large city grew up where the assimilated Jew tried to mask his business. If the Jew was not distinguished by his clothes or his language and if he endeavoured to keep as many Poles as possible in his store, the illusion was created that he could grow into the Polish environment, which had the power in its hands to determine the future of the whole country.

In industry, the situation was a little different but essentially the same. Jews constituted a large percentage of owners—in the Bialystok textile industry over the past 20 years, they made up 100% of factory owners.

However, Jews made up only a small minority of all people employed in industry, including workers, and could have been barely visible among the mass of non-Jewish workers. That, at any rate, appears to be the case if one does not investigate their actual social situation. Doing so reveals that in this economic branch, too, Jews were not integrated into the surrounding sea of Poles but formed a Jewish industrial ghetto.

Jewish workers were distributed thusly according to the 1931 census: 82% were employed in craft work and small industry, 15% in middle-size industrial establishments and only 3% in large industrial plants. Among non-Jews the situation was completely different. More than 37% of Polish workers were employed in large industrial plants, more than 20% in middle-size industrial establishments and 42% in craft work and small industry.

Since Christian owners in Poland did not employ any Jewish workers whatsoever, Jewish craft work and Jewish small industry was, if not one 100%, then at least 90% concentrated in the Jewish quarter of the city, in the Jewish ghetto. In Warsaw, for example, there were many Jewish and non-Jewish tailors and carpenters. The Jewish tailors and carpenters were concentrated in the Jewish part of the city, the Christian tailors and carpenters in the Polish part. Jewish owners employed some Christian workers in the Jewish ghetto, but no Jewish workers were employed in the Christian part of the city. Thus, segregation existed here too. The few Christian workers in the Jewish ghetto adapted to Jewish life insofar as they were members of Jewish unions and participated in union meetings, but the great majority of Jewish workers remained in an isolated Jewish environment.

In Warsaw, which had a big metal industry, there were thousands of Jewish metal workers, but few of them were employed in the big factories, where they would have had to learn the Polish language and customs and adapt to the Polish environment. They worked in small workshops, where they formed the great majority and therefore did not need to adapt to a foreign environment. Some Jewish-owned middle-size and large enterprises employed non-Jewish and Jewish workers. The latter represented only a tiny percentage of the Jewish working class and formed only a minority in their places of work. They were often members of the Polish unions and participated in their meetings, but they made up a tiny percentage and could not erase the national isolation and the avowedly national character of the Jewish working class as a whole.

The Jewish working class was very radical—their socialism was very internationalist, militantly opposed in principle to Jewish traditions and national legacies—but nonetheless bound to Jewish national life forms and Jewish religious traditions because it was almost entirely segregated. A survey conducted among working youth belonging to the Bund, whose program was openly anti-religious, showed that more than one-half of them prayed daily. The stubbornly religious environment proved stronger and more influential than the party program and agitation.

Unorganized Jewish workers were even more nationally traditional, notwithstanding their radicalism as expressed in their voting or social demands and struggles. There existed a big contradiction between supporting a left-wing socialist and fasting on Yom Kippur and Tisha B'Av, but in the life of the Jewish working class in Poland such occurrences were daily phenomena.

The more than 200,000 independent Jewish craft workers were even more isolated from the surrounding non-Jewish world. They were 100% and absolutely in all respects—professionally, socially, politically, culturally, linguistically, and geographically—isolated from their Christian counterparts. This class was largely concentrated in the ghetto and associated almost completely with other Jews. In small towns they did work for people placing individual orders but in big cities they did work for Jewish-owned stores. They bought raw materials from a Jew, borrowed money from a Jewish bank, and sought cures from a Jewish doctor. They read a Jewish newspaper and attended a Jewish theatre, not to mention religion, which was the highest barrier between Jews and non-Jews, especially among members of the Jewish *petite bourgeoisie* such as craft workers and small storekeepers. This environment was the most conservative, not only in religious matters but also in language and culture, because one depended on the other: the more religious, the more nationalistic, the more bound not just to religious holidays and customs but also to Jewish national life forms and manners.

This picture of Jewish socio-economic isolation could be seen clearly in Poland's cities on the very eve of the present war because the penetration of Jewish workers in large industry proceeded terribly slowly and only very gradually changed the general physiognomy of the historically rooted Jewish economic environment. Living in densely populated ghettos, the large *petit bourgeois* mass of storekeepers and craft workers with their salesclerks and journeymen, who, together, made up no less than 80% of Polish Jewry, created the national style of Jewish life in Poland.

Over the last few decades, in trade, crafts, and especially industry, spatial and social sectors formed where Jews met and came into closer contact with non-Jews in the same branches of the economy. This was especially the case for workers in middle-size and large industry and factory owners, the latter of whom sometimes formed business trusts and partnerships with non-Jews and came into contact with them in industry and trade associations. Because of the government's discriminatory policies there emerged a tendency among the Jewish *haute bourgeoisie* to recruit Polish partners in order to save their enterprises from high taxes or allow them to obtain export or import licenses. However, these few points of contact did not determine the physiognomy of the Jewish majority. The isolating barriers that resulted from centuries of organic development were determinate.

Occupational separateness enriched and deepened residential segregation, laying the groundwork for a distinctly Jewish social differentiation and a nationally coloured economic environment, almost a unique economic unity. The Jewish socio-economic environment in the big cities gave rise to nearly independent institutions; Jews performed almost all functions, from the noblest to the hardest and most poorly paid. If in the Jewish ghettos the night watchmen were Christians, it was not because there were no Jewish candidates for this most difficult and poorly paid job but because the government wanted its own people in every courtyard, and every watchman was also a secret police agent.

The 50,000 Jews in crafts and small industry in Warsaw or the 30,000 in Lodz worked only for Jewish employers who purchased their raw materials and sewing accessories only from Jews, sold their manufactured goods almost entirely to Jewish storekeepers from the same city or province and borrowed money only from Jews or from Jewish cooperative funds. As a consumer, the Jewish worker purchased only from Jewish storekeepers and craft workers. And this all took place in a spatially segregated district with its own newspapers and theatres, houses of prayer and study, Hasidic houses of prayer, synagogues and teachers, *yeshivas* and *cheders*, tens of Jewish economic, political and cultural organizations and unions. This environment, laden with religious and national content, influenced the mind and the spirit of the Jewish worker much more than did the pamphlet's internationalist socialist agitation. This environment exerted an even more conservative influence on the large *petite bourgeoisie*, no member of which endeavoured to tear himself away ideologically from his ghetto roots. However much modern life demanded new ways of living, new ideologies, new fundamental beliefs and cultural tendencies, they grew up from the old ways of living and as a natural continuation of them. Therefore, there was no sudden jump from the ghetto to a completely foreign world, no sudden discarding of the entire historical legacy onto the garbage heap, no instant inner and outer metamorphosis, no uprooting from the ground such as took place in other countries.

D. Political segregation

One must add socio-political isolation to the geographical and socio-economic segregation of Polish Jewry. Not only was it impossible for Polish Jews to be active in non-Jewish political parties (which was possible even in Tsarist Russia); they were also in separate economic organizations.

Where there are large Jewish masses, it is natural for Jewish political parties and social and economic organizations to spring up. That was the situation in Tsarist Russia and at one time in Austria. But in both those countries there were parts of the Jewish population, especially among the intelligentsia, who found it more appropriate and comfortable to join the political parties of the majority. Most of them were highly assimilated Jews or those for whom the small Jewish street was simply too narrow. Jews were very active for many years in the Polish Socialist Party, which played the main role in the freeing of Poland. {Herman} Diamand and {Hermann} Lieberman were for many years the representatives of the Polish working class in the Austrian parliament.[18] For tens of years, Felix Perl was editor of the official organ of the socialist party. But in Poland there was not one liberal bourgeois

---

18 {When Galicia was part of the Austro-Hungarian Empire.}

party such as the Kadet {Constitutional Democratic} Party in Russia in which Jews could be active. Even the Polish Socialist Party, which had to take the atmosphere into account in independent Poland, made less of an effort in recent years to put Jews in responsible posts, deciding *de facto* that Jews should not join the party in large numbers. This does not mean that the Polish Socialist Party was antisemitic. To the contrary, it energetically fought against antisemitism. However, taking account of the sentiment among the masses, it considered it politically more expedient that Jews should join the Jewish socialist parties rather than a general but essentially Polish party.

From the Jewish national standpoint, it was desirable that Jews, including workers, should be concentrated in Jewish political parties. From a political standpoint, however, it was very important for Jews, as a minority, to have representatives in the general political parties; they served as very useful ties between the Jewish and non-Jewish population. They were often the best clarifiers and defenders of Jewish interests in the surrounding political environment. In Russia, {Maksim Moiseevich} Vinaver played this role in the Kadet Party and {Leon} Bramson in the Folkist Party. In Poland, this kind of connecting member was entirely lacking.

Even more important was isolation in economic organizations. Jewish and Polish merchants were in separate associations. The same was true for small traders, craft workers and home workers. Even workers' unions were separate although they were all socialist.

For a time in the liberal professions, there were common organizations, but national competition quickly overcame common professional interests, so Jewish doctors, engineers, technicians, and dentists were forced to establish their own purely Jewish associations.

We can create the following scale of the influence of national competition and antagonism on various social groups in Poland. The influence of the national contradiction was weakest among workers, among whom common class interests always overcame their nationalist antithesis. The national contradiction was stronger among craft workers and still stronger among small storekeepers and market traders. It was strongest and sharpest among members of the intelligentsia, who were in Poland (and perhaps not just in Poland) the most active carriers of antisemitism. The one group in Poland where common class interests overcame national antagonism was the urban *haute bourgeoisie*. In this upper economic circle, the talent of the person and the prospects of the business are what mattered. However, this group was too small to have much influence on the situation of the country's Jews.

In sum, the national development of Polish Jewry was a result of a whole complex of factors, both of a positive and a negative character. Population density and social concentration created a sound foundation for independent life forms and distinct cultural creations. The repelling forces of the surrounding Polish world did not allow assimilation processes to develop and prevented the dismantling of the Jewish ghetto and the weakening of Jewish forces.

Nonetheless, in Poland, too, assimilative forces were at work, tearing through all barriers and leaping over all fences. But before we review this dynamic side of Jewish life in Poland we must consider some historical factors that made the Polish-Jewish public relatively stable, immune to assimilation and capable of resistance.

E. The influence of heritage

The national-religious heritage of Polish Jewry helped to ensure that the community would splinter less as a result of the assimilative forces of the nineteenth century, preserving its organized national character more deeply and longer than in the West.

Polish Jewry had lived an organized, autonomous life for centuries. Jews in many countries had autonomous religious communities, but nowhere else were they so broadly organized in districts, centralized across the entire land and laden with as many social, financial, cultural and religious functions as the Polish *kahal*. This alone had a colossal influence on national consolidation and unified discipline. In Poland, autonomy—the historical surrogate for Jewish life organized by means of a state—approached the highest stages of development.[19]

---

19 {Local *kahals* originated in the 1500s. From the second half of the sixteenth century until 1764 they were overseen by the Council of Four Lands in Lublin, a central body with 70 representatives from local *kahals*. Poles commonly called the Council the Jewish Sejm, or parliament. *Kahals* were abolished by the Tsar in 1844 but most of their functions continued to be performed in the Russian Empire by local synagogue supervisory boards. *Kahals* were not abolished in the Hapsburg Empire.

Jews in the diaspora feel more like scattered individuals than part of a nation; mainly they feel like members of a local community. We are not speaking here about the marginal remains of inherited religious or national feelings. Nor are we speaking of catastrophes that suddenly make every Jew sense his group membership. Rather, we have in mind the concrete, daily dependence of members of the national group on one another, the normal, healthy feeling of belonging that is a product of mundane common interests and experiences, common earthly goals and aspirations. All these concrete daily source of cohesion removes the sense that one lives in a foreign city, a foreign state. National Jewish cohesion among members of the Jewish population in normal times and under normal conditions is only an incidental phenomenon that grows when pogroms, slaughters, acts of violence and incidents of persecution befall the Jews; and it is their "good fortune" that such occurrences repeat themselves with an historical regularity that is seldom seen in the history of other peoples.

Jewish autonomy in Poland could not entirely replace a territory and a state, which create the normal and healthy feeling of cohesion and collective emotion that we spoke of earlier. However, it was so encompassing and enduring, and of such concrete and variegated content in the daily lives of Polish Jews that it exerted an intensive influence and made deeper imprints in their souls than was the case for Jews in other countries.

Enjoying broad administrative-regulatory, socio-economic, financial-fiscal, religious-cultural and educational functions, the autonomous organs nurtured in Polish Jews a deeper consciousness of being tied to the community, of obligation to be concerned for the welfare of the community and to bear the yoke of its continued existence—a deeper and healthier source of national cohesion than that brought about by inertia or catastrophic shocks.

It is enough to mention only the network of educational institutions, from elementary *talmud-torahs* to the most advanced *yeshivas*, that were the responsibility and were funded by local or central organs, to gain an impression of the great influence that these organs must have had on the entire Jewish population. The central autonomous organs supported the

---

Consequently, they were able to re-emerge in independent Poland after World War I.}

founding of presses in Krakow and Lublin because private enterprises were not profitable. They supported an entire staff of itinerant preachers and interpreters who spread Torah and Jewish knowledge among the masses and taught them good character traits. Not only did these autonomous organs support some writers, enabling them to publish their books, but they obliged each *kahal* to buy a certain number of *gemoras*,[20] depending on the number of families in the community. Houses of prayer and study were required to have a certain number of religious books available to all who entered. A community of 50 householders was obliged to support the learning of 30 young men. The *kahal* supported the *yeshivas*, and there was a law that the head of the *yeshiva* should be supported so he would have no material worries and would be able to run the *yeshiva* with a calm head and study Torah "day and night." This widely branched education system was not just for children but also for adults, and its remnants were still pronounced among Polish Jewry even in recent years, directed by the publicly recognized organs that functioned for centuries and left a deep impression on the soul of Polish Jewry—an impression of national organization and responsibility, of national loyalty and consciousness, national devotion and sacrifice.

National education in general—and especially among a people without a country—is the most important and influential factor in generating and preserving national consciousness. So long as the old, deeply national education system was dominant among Polish Jewry, there was no sign of assimilation. The segregated, independent education system created a cultural barrier between Jews and non-Jews, a *conditio sine qua non* for one's own national culture. Even if all other factors keeping the Jewish population apart continue to operate, when this barrier falls their influence ceases to foster national creativity and productivity.

F. The crisis

Two main factors, one conditioning and completing the other, were in the past few decades responsible for creating cracks and holes in the spatial and economic unity and the national-cultural creativity of Polish

---

20 {The *gemora* is second part of the Talmud, consisting of rabbinical analysis and commentary on the first part, the *mishna*.}

Jewry: capitalist differentiation and the decline of the Jewish educational system.

Over the past 70–80 years, capitalist development ripped parts of Polish Jewry out of the previously sealed collectivity. A Jewish *haute bourgeoisie* emerged. It founded the first banks in Poland and financed the first railroads in the country, tying together the Polish, Russian and international markets. Welcomed with joy and pride, its first generation was quickly torn away from the Jewish economic organism and absorbed into the surrounding Polish society and culture. It was only natural. The economic role of this Jewish class—in banking, railroad construction, sugar and tobacco factories and so on—was too responsible and lofty not to strive to adopt the physiognomy of the majority population, especially because liberalism was then dominant, and hopes were high for emancipation by means of assimilation.

Parallel with, and partly also as a result of, capitalist development, the Jewish professional intelligentsia began to emerge. From its origins, it based its perspective and its ambitions not on the narrow and one-sided economy of the Jewish ghetto but on the expanding needs of the entire country, and therefore in the first place on the Polish majority. This group was welcomed early on by young Polish society with sympathy and friendship.

These two new Jewish groups—the richest and the strongest—began advocating modern, secular education, which then meant rejecting Jewish education, which was strictly religious and thoroughly conservative at the time. It also meant separation from the entire Jewish world because secular education then involved learning the country's language, culture and rites.

The emergence of these two groups took place in the first quarter of the nineteenth century. Only after the 1860s, when capitalist development began sinking deep roots in Poland, did they take on a more or less mass character that was able to crack ossified Jewish life.

The great majority of Polish Jewry remained spatially and economically isolated, undergoing capitalist development within its own historically-crystallized ghetto. The one-sided, monochromatic Jewish trade and tavern environment of the eighteenth century broke up and became differentiated. New social classes and strata emerged, notably a middle *bourgeoisie* and a proletariat, the latter consisting of people who now had few opportunities to become owners. The old classes assumed a modern face, adapting to the demands of the new era.

All this occurred mainly within the Jewish environment. However, the above-mentioned upper classes, although consisting of few people, were highly influential, drawing to them the sympathies and aspirations of a far broader circle. They revolutionized Jewish life, tearing pieces from it and planting them in the outside world.

Gravitation to the ideas of the two upper classes, of being elevated to a higher rung, did not affect only the Jewish middle *bourgeoisie* but also much broader strata. Rising to the *haute bourgeoisie* was often impossible, but it was much easier to become a physician or a lawyer. This meant learning a foreign language and a foreign culture.

The development of large cities was also highly influential in this regard. They gave rise to a new type of customer, the national customer. Intellectuals, office workers, even average big-city dwellers are more nationalistic than rural folk. The school, the newspaper, the theatre and in recent years the cinema and radio are robust nationalizing factors even if they do not set themselves nationalistic goals.

The development of national consciousness for the majority means a loss of national consciousness for the minority. Whoever wants the new type of customer must be more or less like him in language, manners and appearance, and must adapt to his days of rest and forego the Sabbath and his own holidays. The Jewish storekeeper on a central street in a large city must appear completely different that his counterpart in the small town or the countryside, who deals only with rural consumers. In the ghetto, the Jewish storekeeper or the better craft worker dreams of extracting himself from the narrow Jewish streets and opening a business or workshop in the central part of the city, where his prospects are much better. While still in the ghetto, he starts preparing himself in terms of language and appearance for a place in the new, growing market in the city centre. And if he himself has no hope of opening such a store in the city centre, he at least prepares his children for a life outside the ghetto. This means speaking Polish to them and making certain exceptions on the Sabbath and holidays. Some do so with a light heart and others with heartache, but in recent years, even on Nalewki Street in Warsaw, one began to see Jewish stores open for business on the Sabbath.

Simultaneously, Polish competition began to grow rapidly. Small Polish food shops grew into large grocery businesses, and the children of rich Polish grocery store owners started opening haberdasheries and textile stores. Children of better-off Polish peasants and skilled workers no longer all went to work in the factories. They already had an urban education, bigger appetites and higher ambitions. Some became office workers and many were drawn to all branches of trade and craft work. Jews originated and developed these two sectors in Poland, and after decades of involvement, Poles in craft production and trade still remained a minority. Yet, from the beginning, they considered themselves to be the bosses, privileged and preferred. From the beginning they proclaimed a struggle against the Jews, who "grabbed" control of craft production and trade. The entire, nearly completely independent Jewish economic structure began to tremble.

Most Jews remained in the ghetto and began creating defensive positions such as their own credit associations offering inexpensive credit for those in need, but the situation kept on changing. The proportion of Jews in the cities started falling as the influx of non-Jews began to overtake the inflow of small-town Jews. Over the last 20 years, once the Poles achieved political independence, they used their political power widely in the economic struggle. They used all means, kosher and non-kosher, to pull and drag Poles into the cities so as to replace their Jewish character with a Polish face. They tried to Polonise not only cities in Polish districts but also in Ukrainian and White Russian districts. It was not just the government that worked toward that end, but Polish society. An organization was founded in Posen to make inexpensive credit and subsidies available to Poles who migrated to Ukrainian and White Russian districts.

Although Jews remained a majority in many branches of trade and craft production, they nonetheless had to adapt to the population majority, from which their strongest competitors came. There may be just one Polish store for every three Jewish ones, but the Polish store was the strongest and dictated its national role. It did not remain quiet and wait for customers and did not compete on the quality or price of goods. Instead, its owners shouted at the top of their lungs that it is the foundation of the Polish state and the saviour of the country's Polish heritage and appealed to all true patriots not to weaken their conscience by buying from a Jew. In such a situation it was natural that among members of the Jewish middle class, most of whom were still in the ghetto, a tendency emerged to adapt to the language and appearance of the majority, hoping that by this means they would be able to endure and save themselves from the patriotic pounding on their heads.

All these processes took on clear contours in the last quarter of the nineteenth century, ushering in a new era in the life and destiny of Polish Jewry. But in independent Poland they assumed dangerous forms. It would be laughable if it were not necessary to cry over the fact that the more menacing the tactics of the emerging Polish trade elements to displace Jews became—from inexpensive credit for Polish storekeepers to picketing and assaulting Jewish storekeepers—the more the Jewish ghetto lost its Jewish character, the more Jews tried to adapt to the surrounding Polish world. Every Jew continued to hope that by acting in this manner they would save their economic position. Assimilation thus took on tragic forms. There were no illusions about actual emancipation, of integration into Polish society, of education and respect for humanity, as in Western Europe. Assimilation in Poland was not demanded by a surrounding non-Jewish world promising freedom and equality in exchange. It was assimilation based on fear, driven by the whip of non-Jewish competitors, who shouted that the assimilated Jew is no more agreeable than the beard-and-sidelocks Jew.

And so, in independent Poland, a woeful situation emerged. Spatial socio-economic and socio-political barriers between Jews and non-Jews remained. They grew higher because the atmosphere beyond the ghetto walls became laden with such bitter hatred that many non-Jews who had left the Jewish city quarters had to return to the ghetto. Cultural barriers began to crumble a little. The ghetto lost its former unity and strength, and with them its creativity and distinct flavour. The ghetto did not disappear as in Western Europe after emancipation. It was shredded from the inside. Jewish culture was not replaced by a foreign culture. Rather, a sort of cultural synthesis was taking place.

Until the beginning of the nineteenth century, probably 99% of Jewish children in the world received a national-religious education. The religious barrier between Jews and non-Jews was thick and high, so when Jews learned a new language in the process of externally adapting to a foreign environment, they filled the new language with so much national-religious content at home that it became a new Jewish dialect. Transitioning to the new language never involved accepting a foreign culture because that was possible only with conversion and leaving one's people entirely. Points of contact always existed with aspects of the surrounding culture, but the roots of Jewish culture always remained firmly planted. Only rarely did they grow over the boundaries permitted by religious Jewry. The type of Jew who grew into a foreign language and culture heart and soul, for whom the foreign language dominated and who dreamt only the dreams of a foreign people yet remained formally a Jew—this atypical Jew was a child of the secular epoch of the nineteenth century.

Polish Jewry had a long sojourn in the country. It was intimately connected with the Polish landscape. It was continuously involved in economic activities that brought it into daily contact with the surrounding population. One-third of the Jewish population had for centuries dotted the countryside as two or three families in a sea of Poles or Ukrainians. Nonetheless, it fostered and developed the dialect it brought from Germany, transforming it into a national language. On the ground of historical Poland this dialect grew into a national instrument which in the recent period played a colossal role in Jewish cultural development.

In every country, with the entry of the first Jewish child in a foreign school, assimilation really begins. Through the school, the Jewish child becomes joined to the foreign language not just superficially but intimately, in spirit. In the youngest, most impressionable years, the Jewish child is pulled into the sphere of the foreign culture, which delights and charms precisely the most capable children, those blessed with refined sensibility and rich imagination.

This assimilation process began in Poland at the very beginning of the nineteenth century. Because Poland was then divided among three countries (Germany, Austria and Russia) and subject to two foreign languages and cultures (German and Russian), assimilation did not quickly become a big influence on the Jewish population. In Posen, the German language achieved dominance over the Jewish population, and the majority migrated to Germany. In Austrian Poland, too, the German language competed with Polish, but the latter won out. In Russian Poland, there was no public school, either Polish or Russian, so the influence of assimilation was weak.

Even in these persistently difficult circumstances, assimilation managed to tear away at a large part of the Jewish intelligentsia, which dived into Polish culture and became organically connected to it. Significant Polish poets and belletrists who occupied prominent positions in Polish literature emerged, not to mention scientists in all fields. It is enough to recall the poet, Julian Tuwim, who was considered the greatest Polish poet of his time, and the belletrist, Józef Wittlin, whose work was published in America. There were many other less illustrious Jewish poets and novelists in Polish literature.

Parallel with this assimilated intelligentsia, the Yiddish ghetto produced a Y. L. Peretz, a Sholem Asch, a Hersh Nomberg, a Yosef Opatoshu, an Isaac Bashevis Singer, a Zusman Segalovitch and tens of other writers of great heft. A network of national cultural institutions that would be a source of pride for any people in its own land was also created.

The situation became completely tragic in independent Poland. Thanks to the growth of the Polish middle classes and the most intense antisemitism, the ghetto began to grow, and with it, isolation. Nonetheless, the tempo of linguistic and cultural assimilation increased. It had nothing in common with nineteenth century Western European assimilation because there could no longer be any talk of growing into Polish culture. The pushback from Polish society simply became too strong. The atmosphere became so poisoned that the most brilliant Jewish child, knowing the Polish language as well as possible, could not grow up to become a Polish poet like Tuwim did 30 or 40 years earlier. However, superficial assimilation was sufficient to interfere with the unity of the Jewish cultural edifice, to weaken the creative zest of the Yiddish-speaking wing that had only just begun to deploy its creative forces. How could this occur amidst strengthened and more extensive spatial and socio-economic isolation?

First, because modern forms of culture jump over the highest barriers and tear into the most fenced-in and remote Jewish homes. The radio, the gramophone and the cinema all assimilate. The distinctive Jesuit school policy of the Polish government played a much larger role. On the one hand, Jewish children had to attend elementary school, and this was very often a Polish public school. On the other hand, Polish Jewry created a large network of national schools with Jewish and Hebrew as languages of instruction. Nearly 200,000 Jewish children, about 40% of all school-age Jewish children, attended these schools and thus remained isolated from the foreign environment and assimilation. Of course, these schools had to teach all the Polish and general subjects, and the Polish government increasingly forced these schools to expand the influence of the Polish language. Nevertheless, a larger percentage of children received a Jewish education than was the case in any other country. Impoverished Polish Jewry spent 20 million *zloty* annually on Yiddish education, almost as much as wealthy American Jewry, which is 50% more numerous.

All the promises and commitments to give minorities, including the Jews, national schools with instruction in their mother tongue were in fact dismissed by all Polish governments, who persecuted the minority schools, especially the Jewish ones. The elementary education of a large percentage of Jewish children in the Polish language was by itself enough to undermine the dominance of Yiddish that existed just a few decades previously. The tragedy was that the same Polish power that dragged Jewish children into general schools blocked the doors of the high schools and universities to them. Assimilated Jewish youth thus remained frozen out of both cultures.

Here one must state that Polish Jewry was nonetheless the strongest fortress of our national values. Around 58% of Polish Jews still lived in the provinces, where Jewish customs, such as those accompanying Sabbath and the holidays, completely dominated; where the living Yiddish language and the modern Hebrew language inspired all Jewish youth; and where the national movement in all its forms dominated the minds of the entire Jewish population. And even in the larger cities, the traditions of Sabbath and the holidays and the use of Yiddish were strong enough. The Polish Jew did not surrender quickly, demonstrating instead a wonderful stubbornness even in his manner of dress. His strong will to be different and not to dissolve into the surrounding population even outwardly manifested itself at every turn. These inherited traits were strong even among big-city Polish Jews. Large parts of cities like Warsaw and Lodz appeared more Jewish than any city quarter with a large mass of Jews anywhere else in the world. The traditional long black caftan that shouted out the distinctiveness of the Jewish people and intentionally demonstrated their readiness to suffer for being a Jew was dear not only to the older generation but also to a large part of the younger generation, which could never be ashamed by comparison with Jewish youth in modern dress, even with respect to their general education, not to mention their Jewish knowledge. Polish Jews stood only at the beginning of their struggle for their own life forms in an environment that wanted to denationalize but not assimilate them. And by its traditions, its national stubbornness and loyalty, Polish Jewry was the most capable of working out methods of national life in the diaspora and serving as an example to all other Jewish communities.

We write in the past tense. Will Polish Jewry remain something in the Jewish historical past? Here we stop. May history, that capricious player with destiny, provide an answer...

2. The birth pangs of the Jewish working class

The birth pangs of the Jewish worker were and remain until now much more severe than those of the surrounding peoples. If physical labour in general was for hundreds of years a curse and an embarrassment in a Jewish family, then working for someone else, an owner, was a double curse and a double embarrassment. Even now it is considered a misfortune, a tragedy for a Jewish boy or girl. One is often prepared to work more and earn less to remain at home working for oneself.

The former peasant who arrives in the city and knocks on the factory door has worn the landowner's yoke for centuries. He arrives with a healthy body hardened by physical labour and with a soul that has for centuries absorbed subjugation and submission. Having an owner over him, a master one must satisfy, is customary. In contrast, the Jew arriving from a small-town home, the home of a minor storekeeper or broker, a cantor or a beadle, a matchmaker or a person with an undefined occupation living hand to mouth, or even a self-employed tradesman—such a Jew brings with him to the city not only a weaker body but also a mentality that is poorly suited for dependent work, a mentality that resists disciplined, mechanized factory labour. And if in a certain country factory production and home industry appear simultaneously before two work-seeking masses, one consisting of rural peasants and the other of small town mercantile elements, then the latter will certainly choose home industry, which at least offers a modicum of independence and much more hope of improving oneself and hauling oneself up to the level of an owner.

Physically and psychologically, the two work-seeking masses were so different that their paths had to diverge. If one adds to this the cultural distance that separated them as well as their linguistic differences, we arrive at two completely different worlds. Social destiny later brought them together, but in the beginning of their struggle for employment in nascent industry it must have felt that they were more divided than unified.

For the factories, especially those owned by Christians, the rural non-Jewish peasant with his healthy body and primitive mentality, trifling needs and even more trifling ambitions, was much less expensive and easier to employ than the small-town Jewish *petit bourgeois* mass with its weak body and excitability; with its higher standard of living and more developed mind; with its oversized interest in the mechanism of the enterprise and ready grasp of the cogs of that mechanism; with its emotional liveliness and mental activity; with its striving to free itself as quickly as possible from the worker's yoke and work its way into the owners class; with its immense drive to become independent, to organize, to create, to manoeuvre, and to accomplish.

If the pauperized peasant masses entered the wide factory doors of large industry, then some of the pauperized small-town Jewish masses squeezed into the offices of the large Jewish-owned factories, where they found better working conditions and more opportunities for upward mobility than in the factory itself. Many more such Jews

Fig. 2 *Brzeziny. A portrait of a tailor and six members of his family, together at work* (undated), Brzeziny, Poland. ©Archives of the YIVO Institute for Jewish Research, New York, http://polishjews.yivoarchives.org/archive/index.php?p=collections/controlcard&id=22480

threw themselves into expanding craft work production and similar home industry. They had strong ties to, and shared traditions with, the latter two branches in the big cities. In those branches they faced less competition than they did in the factories from the physically stronger and culturally less developed peasants. In the springtime of Polish industry, earnings in craft work and even in home industry were higher than in the factory. The *work* regime was not so hard on the undisciplined and individualistic *petit bourgeois* mentality. Finally, the prospects for tearing oneself away from the yoke of physical labour and jumping into the ranks of ownership were much greater.

The narrow doors of craft work and home work could not permit the entry of all the pauperized *petit bourgeois* Jews who were compelled to do physical labour. However, the workers' struggle brought about a more significant improvement in working conditions in the large factories than in the types of industry that came to be known as "Jewish," the chief feature of which became the sweating system.[1] Jewish craft workers therefore tried to enter large industry. However, they found the factories filled with an ethnically unified mass of workers that was difficult to penetrate. It was hard for the individual Jewish worker, a stranger speaking a different language and having different life habits and manners, to integrate into the homogeneous mass of workers of another ethnicity. Besides, the non-Jewish workers had a strong and persistent kinship with the constant influx of peasants arriving from the countryside; they regarded the newcomers as closer than the alien Jews.

In places like Bialystok, where the Jewish working masses arrived at the right time, before the mechanized textile industry was populated by another ethnic group of workers, and where the effort of Jewish workers to enter large mechanized factories was organized and led by a mass movement, a significant result followed: Jews comprise more than one-half of all weavers working power looms until today. Unfortunately, Jewish workers' organizations did not set themselves the goal of encouraging more Jewish factory employment. More important, the spontaneous drive of the Jewish masses to enter the factories declined in intensity

---

1   {The sweating system involved owners supplying workers with raw materials and paying them by the piece to complete work in their homes or small workshops. It was characterised by long hours, low wages, and unsafe and unsanitary working conditions.}

and stubbornness because of the opportunity to emigrate. In the first quarter of the twentieth century, more than a million Jewish members of the labour force migrated from Eastern Europe to America. For a while, America freed the Jewish masses from their historic necessity not only to transition to physical labour but *to adapt to the working conditions of the majority and make themselves competitive in the labour market.*

However, the material and social improvement that America made possible for millions of Eastern European Jews over a period of half a century has ended. *We now live in an epoch when the broad Jewish masses are forced to adapt to the most difficult conditions of the local labour market. The Jewish masses will have to make their second great effort to become equal to the surrounding population not just in terms of doing physical labour but in terms of working in the same conditions and with the same discipline and orderliness.*

There stands before me a 64-year-old weaver. He works at Trilling's factory. The entire first floor with more than 50 looms is occupied exclusively by Jewish male and female workers. The second floor is occupied exclusively by Christian male and female workers. If a loom is vacated on the Jewish floor, the position is filled by another Jew; if a loom is vacated on the Christian floor, it is filled by another Christian. The 64-year-old weaver with a nice patriarchal beard and a stately appearance unlike that of a worker has been working at a loom for 49 years. He weaves and weaves and remains poor. His parents owned a little tobacco factory. He worked there from the age of 13 to 15. He studied in *cheder* until he was 13 and even now he throws a verse and an aphorism into conversation so one feels he hasn't torn himself away from a Jewish book his whole life. At 15 he became a weaver and started earning 6 roubles a week. That was a time when Bialystok's textile industry was growing and weavers were in demand. Boys poured in from the surrounding towns—children from good, well-off families of storekeepers, merchants and Jewish functionaries—to learn weaving. A few became factory owners. Hundreds remained workers. The industry pulled youth into the city and the factory, ridding themselves of an angry father, a strict teacher and starting a life of earning a living and becoming independent. Even now a fire ignites the eyes of the old man when he relates how at the age of 13 he left his *cheder* and its angry rabbi with his leather whip, and how at 15 he left his parents and started living a free life. One senses from his story how narrow and suffocating it was in the old Jewish family and in the old *cheder*. With extraordinary pride and courage the grey weaver tells how, in 1906, when his boss threw out his handlooms and together with them also wanted to throw out his Jewish workers, the latter barricaded themselves in the factory and proclaimed: "'Only over our dead bodies will Christian workers approach the power looms'....More than 25 years I stood in place by the handloom, giving up my best years, and now they want to throw me out! No! Blood flowed and we succeeded!"

The elderly man has six children, all workers. They became carpenters, weavers, and two girls were seamstresses. One son left eight years earlier for Mexico and became a peddler, but the weaver believes that as soon as he familiarizes himself with the country his son will leave the odious peddler role and resume his trade as a carpenter. Speaking with this patriarchal Jewish weaver one feels that here a Jewish work tradition is being created. Manual work is becoming deeply rooted and valued. The inherited chain of doings and dealings, and the notion that "Torah is the best merchandise," is being broken.

And now we are in the home of a *loynketnik*.[2] He sits at a table in a small room reading Henryk Sienkiewicz[3] in Yiddish. In one corner, a stove. In the middle of the room, a table. Around the table are four simple long benches. On the wall are two pictures—Dr Herzl and Medem.[4] Near the window hang a pair of *tefillin* {phylacteries}. Filling a second small room are two beds. To reach the second bed one must crawl over the first one, which stands right beside the door—more accurately beside the hole, because there is no door. The weaver is 57 years old. His parents lived in the countryside, ran a tavern, and traded in grain. In his young years, he studied in a *yeshiva* and knew *gemora* quite well but after that, when they ruined his father's business and took away his tavern, he was forced to go to work. He became a weaver, like many Jewish youth. He worked himself up and before the war he had five of his own looms and employed three workers.

---

2   {A piece worker who spins thread or weaves cloth from material provided by a factory owner. He may own or rent his equipment. He works at home or in a small shop.}

3   {Poland's 1905 Nobel Prize winner in literature.}

4   {Theodor Herzl was the founder of political Zionism, Vladimir Medem the leading theoretician of the Bund, the main Jewish socialist party in Lithuania, Poland, and Russia.}

The war ruined his business. He was taken into the army. He deserted, had difficulties, suffered, and in the end emerged alive. After much wandering and torment he returned to his family in Bialystok. He had to start again from scratch. He learned how to work a power loom, but it was difficult to rid himself of his poverty. Between 1925 and 1929 he worked an average of four months per year. At the beginning of 1930 he was unemployed for more than half a year. His wife was lying sick, and his last pennies were spent on her.

His dwelling is wet and cold. When he works six days a week he earns 42 *zloty* per week. As an unemployed person he receives government support of 12 *zloty* per week, although they removed him from the list of recipients because he has children who work. He has four sons. One is a Hebrew teacher, a former Zionist. He lived in Israel for several years and came back disappointed. The second son is a carpenter and a communist. The third is an office worker in a business and the fourth is learning a trade. The latter two are Bundists.

All the children read books and newspapers with fluency. The father is the only one who prays. He relates this without anger and without annoyance, and one gets the impression that he himself is not religious but prays only from habit. For that reason, he reads a lot of books. He has read not only all the Yiddish writers but all the works of Tolstoy and Zola that have been translated into Yiddish. The poverty and suffering of such an essentially intelligent man made him a little coarser; his down-at-the-heel appearance conceals his inner intelligence.

And now we are in another weaver's home. He grew up beside a handloom because his father was a weaver too. His grandfather, a religious teacher in a nearby small town, who taught to the age of 75 and "educated many Talmudic scholars." The old man wanted to lure his grandson away from his son the weaver and make him into the kind of man who would follow in his footsteps, but that did not happen. At the age of 14, the grandson ran from the *gemora* to the handloom. It was a period when weavers made a good living, and that is what pulled him into the factory. He worked in one factory for 20 years, lived an intensive political life, and he does not regret leaving the *gemora*. Little of the *gemora* remains in him, and aside from a Yiddish newspaper he reads nothing. Four years earlier, the factory in which he worked for 20 years was relocated to Romania. He did not want to move with it, and for two years he was unemployed. Luckily, his wife is a seamstress and earns 15 *zloty* a week. In 1928 and the first half of 1929 he was able to work and eat to satiety. But he has been unemployed again for the last four-and-a-half months.

His two children are studying in a *talmud-torah*.[5] He considers this a necessity; one cannot leave little children without schooling. In a corner of the home sits the wife's 70-year-old mother. Thin, pale, with parchment skin, more dead than alive, already three-quarters in the hands of the Angel of Death. She moans not with the usual sound but with a thick, heavy, stomach-deep groan. Her groans strengthen the gloom that hangs over the home. Three charity boxes hang on the walls—one in the name of Rabbi Meir Bal-Nes,[6] one for the *talmud-torah* and one for the Novgorod *yeshiva*. These were brought into the house by the old woman.

And now I am in a home where I meet a father and his son, both interesting types. Both are weavers, both *yeshiva* students, and devout until today, people who read and contemplate, living an intense spiritual existence. The father studied in a *yeshiva* until he was 20 years old. But the *gemora* did not help him put potatoes in the pot, as he expressed it, so he became a weaver. In Bialystok, weaving was always considered aristocratic work. The son also studied in *yeshiva* but only to the age of 15, when he also became a weaver. He is well acquainted with the new Yiddish literature and he plays on Peretz's expression that the greater the merchant, the smaller the Jew: "The more work, the less *yeshiva*," he says. The son is already 39 years old and is not just a weaver but also a carpenter. He was already in the land of Israel and learned carpentry for his trip because one cannot earn a living from weaving there.

On the way from Trilling's factory to the area of Jewish poverty I dart into a workshop of Jewish *loynketniks*. There were 20 looms belonging to fifteen people in the workshop; five of the *loynketniks* owned two looms and rented them to others. The workers stopped work and encircled me. Communicating the way they talk is impossible. I witnessed such despondent tears, such heart-rending lamentations, that I departed a broken man.

---

5 {A Jewish elementary school modelled after the *cheder* and preparatory to study in a *yeshiva*.}
6 {A second century miracle worker.}

Here is a young man of 18 years. It is almost impossible to see his eyes; he is thin, short, small, almost without a body. On his head, sparse red hair. He works a rented loom, earning 25 *zloty* a week, ten of which he pays the owner of the loom. His workday stretches sixteen to seventeen hours and he is happy that he has work at all. Work is available at most for only one-half of the year. And the second half? He is unable to answer that question.

And here stands a tall Jew, 38 years old, but already with a lot of grey hair. He has the face of an energetic, talented man. He speaks abruptly. We are lying in a pit, he says. We are burying ourselves. We run, one in front of the other, to the factory owner, each lowering his price, and we pay with blood, working an extra hour, an extra two hours, an extra three hours. If I work 15 hours a day, another works 16 hours a day and yet another works 17 hours a day, doing more for less. Thus, we drive ourselves to the grave, and no one is to blame because all of us are hungry and all of us have children at home. I have five little ones. The man working beside my loom already has six children. How can we think about attaining something, about health, about exploitation, about organization and other such things?

And here a third man speaks up, an elderly Jew, 60-odd years old, who worked more than 40 years at a handloom and for the last few years at a power loom. He is alone, his wife having passed away long ago, his children scattered over the face of the earth—two sons in Russia, who have completely forgotten their old father, one in New York, who remembers his father once in a blue moon and throws something his way, and one, the youngest, in Mexico, but from him there is still no good news. The old man is nonetheless satisfied that after 50-odd years of toil he has some capital, his own power loom. Tens of others like him are jealous. But how does one find work for at least six months a year?

On the side, still and beaten down, separated from the talkative crowd, stands a type who gives the impression of a man without elbows who has relinquished himself to fate without protest or resentment. He is quiet, but his silence arouses one's interest. I find out that he was a good student, a well-mannered young man from a very respectable family. In his twenties, the war made him a homeless wanderer. His parents remain stuck somewhere far away in Russia where the homeless were sent after the war began. He has brothers and sisters somewhere, but he has no connection with them and no address for them, and he does not know who among them remains alive and who was swallowed up by the war, the pogroms, the revolution, the terror, the hunger, the epidemics, and thousands of other calamities that in recent years chased people, especially the Jews. He comes from Grodno. During the war he willingly went to Russia. In 1920, during the Russian famine, he managed to escape across the border. More than once he was in the grip of the Angel of Death but miraculously he tore himself away and dragged himself to Bialystok, where he learned weaving. He is working someone else's loom and earning 15 *zloty* a week, living absolutely alone. He is always silent.

Let us now consider the moods of the Jewish worker and factory owner, moods which clearly indicate that the distance between the Jewish and non-Jewish workers is disappearing. On the one hand, the Jewish worker is changing markedly in his material demands and his psychological position, lowering himself to the position of the non-Jewish majority. On the other hand, urbanized cultural elements are growing among non-Jewish workers, who are beginning to reach the demands and aims of the Jewish worker.

A Jewish owner of a department store in Germany with tens of branches was asked why he did not hire a single Jewish clerk. He answered cynically but accurately as follows:

> Business is business! I need clerks who are immersed in their work when they come into the store, so while they are there they won't have other thoughts. They must have no thoughts about how they can steal out to the library during the day to exchange a book, run to language or other courses right after work, or attend professional or political meetings. We do not need people whose feet are in the store and whose heads are elsewhere! Nor do we need people who stick their nose where it doesn't belong—in the accounts and in the names of the firms that supply merchandise or receive merchandise, who want to know every last detail about the business, who don't want to remain in their proper place and receive only their due. The business needs calm, disciplined, simple people, not people who are intelligent and overly cunning. The Jewish clerk is anything but simple and calm, and he is always thinking about how he can become a boss himself.

Here we have a key to understanding many of the reasons that make the Jewish employee, whether a factory worker in Lodz or a store clerk in

Germany, undesirable. Listen to the words of a Jewish worker in Lodz. At a meeting of several tens of Jewish textile workers, an elderly man who has been working a loom for nearly 30 years said the following:

> In 1905 or 1906, when I started working in the factory, I immediately started organizing the workers for a strike. I had nothing to fear. If they fired me I could stay in my father's home or I could immigrate to America. It is completely different now. The Jew works like the devil. There is no place to move to. These days a father cannot support a son. Getting a position is more difficult for a Jew than for a non-Jew. So today a Jew is afraid of losing his job and tries to protect it more than a non-Jew does. He surrenders, becomes calmer, quieter, dependent. Not long ago I started work in a new factory. The first day the owner called me to the side and said: "I hired you even though you are a Jew. However, see to it..."—he didn't need to finish his sentence. We understood one another, and the factory owner was satisfied.

The non-Jewish worker also changed, but in another sense. He is no longer the peasant from the countryside who is ready to work 12–14 hours a day, lacks cultural needs and is politically passive and psychologically dependent and servile. He has lived in the city for 30 years and is used to better living quarters, a better suit of clothes, a newspaper, a professional union, a movie. He has a child in public school or even a high school. He has children in state or community jobs. He feels like a citizen of his country and his city. He does not want to work more than eight hours a day even if he does piece work. He does not fear unemployment because, firstly, he can count on state support and, secondly, nearly every non-Jewish working-class family has a member in a state or community job—with the railroad, the streetcar company, a municipal enterprise and so on. Unemployment is not as tragic a situation as it is for the Jewish worker, who has no one in a state or community job.

 The life of the entire Jewish family depends completely on the father's earnings. Today's non-Jewish worker is therefore sometimes more audacious than the Jewish worker. Moreover, the Jewish worker feels responsibility for the entire Jewish work force. If one Jew works poorly, employers might soon say that Jews in general are not good workers, that they are lazy. The Jewish worker senses that the owner is keeping an eye on him, examining him, testing him, suspecting him. The owner makes a big fuss over every little thing that would amount to nothing if it concerned a Christian worker and is ready to blame it on Jewish workers in general. The Jewish worker must endure examination in the large factory and he musters all his psychological and physical resources not to fail. He therefore works zealously and submissively. This is a condition that the non-Jewish worker does not know.

Here is what a middling Jewish factory owner in Lodz told me:

> Years ago, there was an interest in recruiting Christian workers and not Jews. In the very large factories that tradition remains, but in the smaller factories Jews are now more readily employed. The Christian worker is lazy—he doesn't want to work overtime and he runs to the inspector to report that a factory is demanding more than eight hours of work per day. He is eager to complete the required 20 weeks of work so he can claim state support as an unemployed person, and he is happy to remain without work and receive state support for months on end. The Jew is more diligent, ready to work 12 hours a day so long as he can earn more. He does not turn so gladly to unemployment support and does not receive it so easily either. He does not count his number of work weeks or demand that he be immediately registered for unemployment insurance. It is easier to get along with the Jewish worker than with the non-Jewish worker, who will immediately denounce his employer to the authorities for failing to register him immediately.
>
> All factory doors are open for the non-Jewish worker as if he is a man of esteemed descent. For the Jewish worker, almost all doors are locked, so he holds on for dear life where he has a job. The non-Jewish worker must be paid in cash while the Jewish worker also takes a promissory note. The Jewish worker is more productive because he wants to earn enough to support his whole family while, among non-Jewish workers, wives and children are more likely to work. The Jewish worker would also immediately send his wife out to work if he could, but in recent years it has been difficult to find jobs, and the Jewish woman is less suitable and less used to working. But in this detail, too, much has changed. The Jewish woman and girl strive to work, and Jewish girls, many of them educated and from good families, now comprise most workers in the new knitting industry. In Lodz and the surrounding towns there are now 300 workshops producing sweaters. More than 90% of the workers are Jews, and there are a lot more female than male workers.
>
> The Jew wants desperately to work. Many are glad to do unskilled labour and do so with blood and sweat just to earn something. Their honourable upbringing means nothing now; just to live like an ordinary person they are ready to work on the Sabbath, on a religious holiday, day and night. A Jew who sets out to do something does it with fire in his belly, and you will see that Jews will also push into the big factories. It

will be difficult, but the world is turning. There is no place to go so they adapt. They are no longer little princes devoted to long years of study, lords of the *gemora*. A new world has been created and the Jews must change. Hundreds and thousands of Jewish boys and girls come to Lodz from the provinces—the boys from the *gemora* and the girls from their mothers' aprons—and after three months one cannot recognize them. They have become different people. They learned to work the sewing machine and a new soul was born. Life tinkers, and it will soon fashion something. Meanwhile it is bitter and dark; everyone wants work and jobs are scarce. Every position for a Jew is obtained with great effort, but things keep moving on, and before my eyes Jewish life has changed a lot, become more gentile, more ordinary, coarser, but also healthier and somehow more respectable. And I'll tell you another secret. I employ only Jewish workers because I think to myself, what good does it do me if the workers hate me both as an owner and a Jew? It is enough that they hate me as an exploiter. I feel somehow more secure and calm with a Jewish worker.

It later emerged that this factory owner was in his youth a member of a Jewish socialist party and is familiar with the painful problems and questions of Jewish economic life in general and the life of the Jewish worker in particular. There a few more Jewish factory owners and workers involved in our discussion but they all agreed that the speaker had correctly characterized the situation and shone a bright light on it.

We let living people speak and we recounted what they said practically word for word. What follows from all this talk? First, the higher cultural position of the Jewish manual worker or salaried employee (his more developed personality and sense of self-worth, his more acute grasp of his class situation, his stronger striving to release himself from the yoke of class subjugation) makes him less desirable in the factory or the business. But, however difficult it becomes to remove oneself from the status of salaried worker, however gloomy the situation of the Jewish masses becomes, there grow among the Jews more elements that are willing to adapt to the cultural situation of the surrounding non-Jewish majority and existing working conditions and demands. On the other hand, the development of the wage workers who dominate the surrounding world ensures that the distance between Jewish and non-Jewish wage workers becomes smaller and smaller.

Second, it is clear that in Poland, where the economic crisis among the Jewish population reached its highest and most tragic level, there occurred a deep rupture in the psychology of the Jewish masses, including that of the Jewish working masses. The drive to large industry and work in general has assumed such a spontaneous character and such massive proportions that it will overcome both internal and external stumbling blocks. The adaptive capacity of the Jewish masses will reveal itself here too, especially when it is spurred on by a need that has almost no equal. And to the degree that the surrounding economic situation will allow it, larger Jewish masses will probably force themselves into new branches of industry and higher industrial forms.

Third, we can acknowledge that the rupture in the psychology of Jewish workers and the drive of the Jewish masses to work have already caused a partial change in the relationship of the Jewish entrepreneur to Jewish labour. Even if a long road remains before Jews enjoy equal rights in large Jewish-owned industry, we are far from the absolute boycott of Jewish work that dominated a few years ago.

3. The heritage of the Jewish factory owner

It is not only Jewish and non-Jewish workers in Poland who come from two completely different social, cultural and status groups. The same holds for owners of enterprises.

In Germany and great Russia, upstart tradesmen and rich traders played a major role in the development of industry. In Poland, these elements played an insignificant role, at least as far as the non-Jews among them were concerned. Until the eve of the war, most Christian entrepreneurs in Poland were landowners or former landowners, senior state office holders or their sons, engineers and jurists—almost all members of the upper classes. They were brought up for many generations in an atmosphere in which they dominated the masses and remained estranged from them. A chasm existed between them and the lower classes. Only rarely was a non-Jewish entrepreneur a former peasant, worker, tradesman or merchant who sprang from the lowest to the highest classes. And if Poles could be found among German weavers in the textile industry, then they were rare exceptions in all other branches of industry.

The origins of the first generation of Jewish factory owners were utterly different. A very small number of them came from the Jewish *haute bourgeoisie* with inherited wealth—bankers, landowners and major merchants. For the most part they came from the same classes that gave birth to the Jewish worker or from adjacent and related classes. There was no cultural chasm, no psychological wall, between the first generation of Jewish factory owners and Jewish workers, as there was between their Christian counterparts. The resulting psychological and cultural proximity and near equality between owners and workers caused the owners to see the workers as competitive threats. This circumstance was perhaps one of the most important factors leading them in due course to reject Jewish workers. Fear of the ambition of Jewish labourers and office workers, who quickly grasped the essence of the business, was not unfounded; we will soon see what a large percentage of Jewish factory owners were formerly office workers or master craft workers in factories.

We analysed biographical materials on more than 100 large and middling Jewish textile manufacturers from Lodz and Bialystok.[1] An interesting picture emerged. Their emergence from classes very close to those from which Jewish workers were recruited stands out surprisingly sharply.

In connection with their cultural environment it is enough to say that 95% of the first generation of Jewish textile manufacturers studied in *cheder*. More than three-quarters ended their education with at least some *yeshiva*. One-third of the large textile manufacturers studied in *yeshiva*. None had any higher secular education. Only eight of 50 large manufacturers attended a secular school, although only a primary school and not a high school. Ten of the 50 received their secular education from private teachers.

Let us now see from what sort of population centres the entrepreneurs came, how they were employed before they became manufacturers and how their parents were employed. Of the 93 large and middling textile manufacturers whose place of birth is known, 74.2% were born in small towns, 8.6% in small cities and 17.2% in large cities.[2] Regarding their former occupations, it is revealing to divide them into two groups, as follows:

Table 5 Former occupations of large and middling Jewish entrepreneurs, percent in parentheses

Former occupations	Large entrepreneurs	Middling entrepreneurs
Office workers, brokers, traveling salesmen	26 (49.1)	19 (47.5)
Merchants, storekeepers	8 (15.1)	2 (5.0)
Rabbis, rabbis in training	5 (9.6)	0 (0.0)
Master craft workers in factories	2 (3.8)	16 (40.0)
Manufacturers	12 (22.4)	3 (7.5)
Total	53 (100.0)	40 (100.0)

1 Based on Lazar Kahan's *Ilustrirter yorbukh far industri, handl un finansn*, Lodz, 1925.
2 Eight in Lodz, four in Warsaw, three in Bialystok, one in Odessa.

The first group consists mainly of office workers, children of small-town businessmen who set out in the world to seek their fortune because there was nothing for them to do in their small towns and their inheritance was too small to be of much help. With gritted teeth and bitter hearts, they first worked for others. They were downwardly mobile or the children of the downwardly mobile, but they had a tremendous amount of energy, agility and stubborn will not to remain employees. They wanted to become independent and they made up nearly one-half of the first generation of middling and large textile factory owners. Of course, these former office workers, brokers and travelling salesmen did not constitute even 1% of all the Jews engaged in these occupations. Thousands dreamt and strived but only a few succeeded—the most talented, the most persistent, often also the most miserly and money-hungry. These entrepreneurs, who had themselves experienced working for someone else as salaried workers and made their way to the highest social rung, yet were so close to the masses, became and remained the biggest opponents of Jewish factory labour. That is understandable. They knew full well how close the Jewish worker often stood to the factory owner not only regarding understanding the technical side but also the whole complicated commercial substance of the enterprise.

There were very few former master craft workers among the early large textile factory owners—just 3.8% of the total—but among middling textile factory owners they constituted fully 40.0% of the total. Together with former office workers, brokers and travelling salesmen, they comprised 87.5% of the middling factory owners. Only 5 (12.5%) were former merchants, storekeepers or men who started out as factory owners right away. In contrast, among the large textile factory owners, the distribution of former occupations is completely different. Nearly 10% had been rabbis or rabbis-in-training. Few had been master craft workers in factories, but 22.4% were factory owners from the outset, starting the enterprise with their own capital. Former merchants and storekeepers, who probably also had some capital, constituted just over 15% of the group.

Unfortunately, we have information on the parents' occupations of only 41 large textile factory owners. The parents of 25 of them (61.0%) had been merchants or storekeepers, 6 (14.6%) had been landowners or bankers, 5 (12.2%) had been manufacturers[3] and 5 (12.2%) had been rabbis or teachers of religion. Only the two middle categories, comprising a little more than one-quarter of the total, can be counted as members of the Jewish *haute bourgeoisie*. The remaining nearly three-quarters were either middling owners or "small people with small aspirations."[4] There is no doubt that the middling Jewish textile factory owners originated in the common people much more often.

To add flesh and blood to the data just cited, we will recount a few short biographies of Jewish pioneers in the textile industry:

- "Israel Poznanski was born in 1883 in Alexander, near Lodz. His father, Kalman Poznanski, was an honest merchant. Israel married the daughter of Moyshe Herts, who was secretary of the Warsaw Jewish Community. Immediately after the wedding, Israel started a small business in Lodz's old city."[5] We leave aside the whole story of how this small storekeeper built up his own gigantic factory structures, palaces and houses, mentioning only that, although the business started sharply declining during the war, the Poznanski factories still employed 4,297 workers in 1929.[6] It is important to add that the success of the owners of this firm occurred during the life of the old Poznanski, who came from a simple but respectable home. During his life, the success of the business was much greater than after his death, when his children took over. They were educated and had completely different ambitions and appetites. They assimilated, and some of them converted.

- "Asher Cohen was born in Lodz in 1870. His father raised him, like all his children, at the bosom of the Torah. He hired the best rabbis and instructors to tutor the young Asher, who was blessed with a good head for the *gemora* and was also a diligent student. His father took great pride in his son who, he believed, was set to become a child prodigy. At sixteen-and-a-half, he was married, becoming the son-in-law of Zalmen Rubin in

---

3   Three textile manufacturers, one soap manufacturer, one manufacturer of spirits.
4   {The quotation is from Sholem Aleichem's portrayal of *shtetl* life in his classic series of that title.}
5   Kahan, 52.
6   Rosset, *Lodz miasto pracy*, Lodz, 1929, 43.

3. The heritage of the Jewish factory owner 49

Tomashev {about 60 km. southeast of Lodz}, an important broker."[7] Omitting the story of how Asher became a *maskil*,[8] learned weaving, founded a firm in partnership with others and became director of a large factory, what is important for us is that 8,500 people now work in Asher Cohen's factories.[9] The one-time student of the Talmud who was on the verge of becoming a child prodigy and then became a *maskil* is now the boss of a whole village of factories and houses with its own railroad and a colossal network of textile enterprises.

- "Markus Zilbershteyn began his career as the rabbi of the first Jewish industrial pioneers. Later, after he received a little secular education, he became a bookkeeper for the German firm, Kindler, in Pabianice {about 15 km. southwest of Lodz}."[10] In 1929, some 1,152 workers were employed in Zilbershteyn's factory.[11]

- "Y. Rosenblat was born in Lodz. His father, who was from the *shtetl* Przedbórz {about 125 km northeast of Katowice} and was a rich *chasid*, owned real estate in the environs of Lodz and some houses in Lodz. The younger Rosenblat had a religious upbringing but tore himself away from the house of prayer and *gemora* at a young age. When he was 18, he began manufacturing." Rosenblat's factories employed 2,551 workers in 1929.

- "The Eitingons received a Jewish *bourgeois* education. They first studied in *cheder* and then in the Orsha municipal school. Naum and Boris, who moved to Lodz, proceeded though all the phases that Lodz residents usually went through. Naum worked in Tzemekh's kerchief factory, starting at the lowest level, and rose higher on life's ladder until he left the firm and founded a kerchief factory in partnership with his cousin, Mikhoel Eitingon, from Moscow. Boris Eitingon,

---

7   Kahan, 64.
8   {A follower of the liberal Jewish Enlightenment.}
9   Rosset, 44.
10 Kahan, 38.
11 Russell, 43.

arriving in Lodz, for a short time worked in his relative's business, but he soon got a post in the distinguished firm of Shtiler and Byelshovski. Thus, both Naum and Boris were at first employees— and now 1,028 workers are employed in the Eitingon and Co. factories.

Fig. 3 Bronisław Wilkoszewski, *Fabryka Tow. Ak. Poznańskiego* [The Poznanski textile factory] (1896), Lodz, Poland. Wikimedia, https://commons.wikimedia.org/wiki/File:Bronis%C5%82aw_Wilkoszewski_%E2%80%93_Fabryka_Tow._Ak._Pozna%C5%84skiego.jpg

Until now we have considered the biographies of large owners in Lodz's Jewish textile industry. Now let us turn to a few biographies of owners who employ 300–400 workers each:

- "Yerakhmiel Lipshitz was born in Ozorkow {about 30 km. north of Lodz}. His grandfather was the rabbi of Ozorkow, and his impressive lineage extended all the way back to the rabbi of Kotzk {the spiritual founder of the Ger *chasidic* dynasty}. His father was a well-to-do glass merchant. At the age of 16, the young Lipshitz moved in with his relative in Lodz, Fayvl Shulzinger, and there graduated from his first "classes" in the "academy of trade." Now Lipshitz owns an enterprise that has all the technical means to produce textiles from raw materials to finished products, including Raschel machines {for making lace}, knitting machines, circular knitting machines, his own weaving shop for making kerchiefs, and his own finishing machines."

- Solomonovitsh was born in Petrikov {about 200 km west of Katowice}. He worked for a few years as a secretary in the wood industry. He married in Tomaszów. His father-in-law was the well-known Tomaszów broker and wood merchant.[12]

- Poretski and Govenski own one of the largest textile enterprises in Bialystok. Poretzky was born in Shtutshin and Govenski in Vasilishki, both in the province of Vilna. Soon after each of them were married, they started trading in wood. While they both founded their company, Poretzky's son was mainly responsible for its development. He arrived in Bialystok in 1896 from a *yeshiva* and became the driving force of the enterprise. Their factory became well known because it was the site of one of the most difficult struggles of Jewish workers for the right to become machine weavers; they were the first to be victorious in this regard, winning the right to occupy one-half of the factory's machine-weaving positions.

- A. and Y. Pikelni came from Novogrodek {about 200 km east of Bialystok}. Their father, a well-known scholar, owned a liquor factory. He was a follower of the Enlightenment and raised his sons accordingly. Avrom Pikelni was the first of the children to leave the town to seek his fortune, and because the family had a relative in Lodz, and Lodz was considered "Little America," he moved there and took a position in the German firm, Josef Richter. A. and Y. Pikelni is now a mechanized weaving company in Zdunska Wola {about 50 km. southwest of Lodz} with 112 looms and a business in Lodz.

- Avrom Moyshe Prusak from the small town of Drobnin in Plotsk province was born in 1820 to a merchant family. He

---

12   These and later biographical details about factory owners are from L. Kahan's book.

arrived in Lodz a young man and immediately took to trade and manufacturing. He was a religious, *chasidic* Jew who regularly sought advice from his *rebbe* and would do nothing without the *rebbe*'s approval. Prusak was among the very first pioneers of mechanized weaving in Lodz. At the time, factory owners and machine weavers were almost all Germans. When Prusak introduced weaving machines, he hired Jewish weavers and taught them machine weaving. This caused an uproar among the German machine weavers. Under the leadership of Julius Heinzel, who was then still a weaver but later became a great industrialist and was given the title of baron, they marched to the Jewish quarter to destroy the Jewish factories. However, the mayor found out about it in time and dispatched Cossacks, who dispersed the German weavers and drove them off.

- Herman Foyst was born in Czestochowa {about 125 km. northwest of Krakow}. At the age of 13 he set out to make a living for himself. He was employed in the office of the Jewish factory owner, Levitski, in Pabianice. He then took a position in the office of the largest factory in Pabianice, owned by the Baruch brothers. A few years after he married, he became a factory owner himself and he is now one of the richest entrepreneurs in Pabianice.

- Sh. H. Tsitron, born in Mikhalovo near Bialystok, was a grandson of the well-known Bodker rabbi and head of the Rozan *yeshiva*. His father had a dry goods store in Mikhalovo. Tsitron studied in *yeshivas* and arrived in Bialystok at the age of 17, where he started trading in cloth. Later he became a factory owner, and is now one of the biggest entrepreneurs in Bialystok.

- Yankev Kahan is known as the "the King of Socks" in Poland. Born in Berezovka near Odessa, where his father had a dry goods store, the young Kahan studied with the best tutors and was considered a genius. At 12 he became an orphan, and at 13 he went to Odessa where he became a sales clerk in a small manufacturing shop. Later he founded a brokerage office in Odessa and then moved to Lodz, where he became a travelling salesman. He then founded a sock factory and became the first person in Lodz to introduce sock manufacturing by machine. He is now one of the biggest sock manufacturers in Lodz. In his younger years Kahan wrote in *Kol mevaser*, *Folksblat*, and Spektor's *Hoyz-fraynd*.

- Y. Sheps was born in Tomashev and as a child was considered a prodigy. As a youngster he became a rabbi in Tomashev and at the age of 15 he was already issuing rulings on religious questions. However, he made a living not as a rabbi but in the wool trade, and from there he transitioned to manufacturing.

- Volf Alt was born in Kovel {about 160 km. east of Lublin}. He arrived in Lodz as a child and completed school there. At the age of 15 he began work at Herman Kahan's factory, where he became a master craft worker. Now independent, he employs 80 workers.

- The Teytelboym brothers were born in Gabin {about 100 km west of Warsaw}. They worked in Voydislavski's factory as master craft workers. Already before the war they had their own factory where they employed 300 workers. Now they employ up to 100 workers.

What do we learn from these biographies? We learn first that all Jewish entrepreneurs began without capital, either inherited or substantial capital of their own making. All of them worked their way up thanks to their intelligence, energy, animated nature and entrepreneurial agility. Almost all Jewish entrepreneurs began putting out goods to be manufactured in people's homes and then, after accumulating a little capital, they founded factories. The origins of nearly all of them were in the Jewish middle class; they came from comfortable homes, but from homes that were downwardly mobile. About half the factory owners went through a stage of working for someone else, for the most part as office workers and sales clerks getting a taste of dependent work, and then they made a transition from poor young Jewish men to major capitalists. Culturally, and almost without exception, they studied in *cheder* and had a traditional Jewish upbringing; they studied *gemora* and many went to *yeshiva*. Most of them received a secular education only when they were grown up, already engaged in life's struggles, often from private tutors, and also not infrequently from self-education.

This is the profile of the first generation of textile factory owners. Clearly, the second generation has a completely different character, having opened a social and cultural gap between themselves and Jewish workers, who, to a considerable extent, are until today recruited from the same strata as the first generation of textile factory owners. However, an even larger proportion of the Jewish working class comes from ruined members of the *petite bourgeoisie* and from the poor masses in general, who live off fortuitous employment and earnings.

The condition of Bialystok industry after the war illustrates the enormous effect of the psychology deriving from these social origins on the development of the new occupations into which Jews have moved. In Bialystok, ownership of the textile industry is now completely in Jewish hands aside from one plush factory belonging to a German. Before the war there were 10 German factory owners and more than 100 Jewish factory owners, including owners who put out goods to be manufactured in people's homes. In 1912, of 66 weaving factories (apart from those where weavers worked with customers' materials), 58 were owned by Jews.[13]

The largest factories were in German hands. The 10 German factories employed about one-third of all textile workers in Bialystok, housed about 25–30% of all looms and were responsible for 40–45% of all textile production. After the war, Bialystok's textile industry experienced considerable shrinkage. On the eve of the war there were 1,500 looms in operation and now there are only 1,000. Production has fallen by 50%. There were 4,675 textile workers in Bialystok in 1895; on the eve of the war about 10,000; in 1920, 5,133; and in 1928, 3,975.[14] Bialystok thus employs fewer workers today than it did more than 30 years ago.

Why did all the German textile enterprises go under while the Jewish ones remained? This is a most interesting chapter of economic history that demonstrates *the great importance of the psychology of various entrepreneurial groups—their entrepreneurial spirit, their stubborn adaptability, their capacity to outlast others and drag themselves through to better times.*

---

13 A. Ziskind, "Fun Byalistoker arbeter-lebn," *Fragn fun lebn*, No. 2–3, 1912.
14 "Di antshteyung, antviklung un matzev fun der byalistoker tekstil-industri," *Yoyvl-zhurnal fun prof. fareyn fun tekstil-maysters in byalistok*, March 1929, 30, 31.

3. The heritage of the Jewish factory owner

Right after the war, the Bialystok textile industry revived a little. The Polish government, which led a war against the Bolsheviks, placed large orders. Later the economic crisis began. With Russia locked shut, it was first necessary to take advantage of the internal Polish market as much as possible, especially the newly integrated areas of Congress Poland. Second, it was necessary to seek new markets wherever possible—in the Far East, China, Japan, the Balkans and Hungary. So long as inflation lasted, and Polish goods were very inexpensive, the German textile factories in Poland continued to produce. But when stabilization occurred, Polish goods were insufficiently competitive. Capital became meagre and there was nowhere to borrow from. However, Jewish factory owners proved themselves wonderfully adaptable.

They sent agents to the farthest points in Asia. Because Russia was closed, they had to travel three months to reach China and the Far East. Goods took 5–6 months to arrive. It took 9–10 months before payment arrived. Some of the large Jewish factory owners themselves went on these long journeys to Asia, struggling to find a market for their goods. For example, blankets from Bialystok became one of the most widespread articles in China and to some degree also in Japan. To a considerable extent they out-competed English goods. After a long struggle in the Balkan countries, Bialystok's Jewish factory owners also captured a significant market share, especially in Romania and Yugoslavia.

It was not easy for them to fund these ventures, but here too they proved themselves adaptable pioneers whom the German factory owners could not match. They started paying workers with six-month or even eight-month promissory notes. The workers had to sell them on the stock exchange. Bills for wagons of goods sent to faraway places were sold to banks, often to the Hamburger Volksbank but not infrequently also to local "percenters" who had multiplied in number throughout Poland. Finally, they simply borrowed money; the Jewish factory owner was not ashamed to borrow small sums from tens of people to put together the capital he needed. Interest-free loans from Jewish charitable organizations as well as loans from Jewish savings and loan associations also helped the Jewish middle and small factory owners.

The scattering of Jews to the ends of the Earth to find new buyers and adapt to the new market, the shipping of entire lots of material and receiving payment only 9–10 months later—this pure Jewish twisting, grabbing, covering, borrowing, patching and always being in a market of payments and obligations without knowing how many hundreds of promissory notes one had signed and when their terms expired (even promissory notes for 20 or 30 *zloty*)—all this without a strict bookkeeping system because one must, after all, economize on administrative expenses—this entire raucous mode of manufacturing was so alien to the German manufacturers that the Germans were forced to completely liquidate their enterprises. In this manner, inherited Jewish agility and adaptability in a moment of hardship became especially important factors in preserving existing positions and capturing new ones.

FOREGROUND

4. National Bolshevism

A few years ago, a Jewish worker from Chicago travelled to Russia to visit and also to familiarize himself with local Jewish life. On the way home he stopped in Berlin and told me the following anecdote. He once sat with relatives and acquaintances from his hometown and they discussed the situation of the Jews in Russia. Suddenly a young man jumped up and ran over to the American, grabbed him by the lapels, and started shouting in a strained voice: "Oy, oy, take me with you to America, take me to New York! At least for one day take me to New York! Just for one day!"

On the question from all sides of what he would do for one day in New York, the young man shouted: "I will climb to the top of the highest tower in New York and scream out to all New York Jews, 'For God's sake, why are you allowing three million Jews to go under? Why are you letting three million of your brothers suffer? Why are you so calm and cold when we are starving, without a shirt on our back?'"

I recalled this incident when I recently departed from Poland. Everyone looked at me with eyes that spoke as if to say that I should climb to the tenth floor and utter a cry about the needs of Polish Jews that would shock everyone to the point that the most coldblooded would be terrified.

Will I succeed in uttering such a cry? Will I actually succeed in providing an accurate picture of the economic life of Polish Jews so that our American brothers will finally realize that we have sinned against Polish Jewry and abandoned them?

I do not want my cry concerning the situation of the Jews in Poland to stir only the hearts of American Jewry. I also want their heads to pay attention, for once to seriously consider not just how to feed the hungry, but how they can be extricated from the conditions in which the number of hungry and naked grow.

One must admit that until now American Jews have seriously occupied themselves with the destiny of Russian Jewry and well understood that it is not enough to send packages of flour and grain or of clothes and shoes, but one must also reconstruct the entire economic life of Russian Jewry and adapt it to the new conditions that have been created there.

The great merit of the emissaries and delegates of the "Joint" and of "ORT"[1] is that they helped so many thousands of Jewish families to settle on the land or become employed in industry. Much greater is their service in being the originators, the initiators, the first to show how to fundamentally reconstruct Jewish economic life. Emissaries have pushed members of the *Yevsektsiya* (the Jewish section of the Soviet Communist Party) and awakened the Soviet government, reminding them that the Jewish question is a state problem, that the Jewish plague is a state plague that must be healed by state ways and means. Accordingly, if in the first years of [agricultural] colonization and industrialization the resources of Jewish societies comprised a large percentage of the expenses toward these ends, they now comprise only a small percentage.

You know very well that in Poland completely different conditions exist, and completely different classes are in power. From this one must absolutely not infer that one must leave the three million Polish Jews to their own devices and refrain from any action. To the contrary, one must infer that it is necessary to formulate a *different* program of work and find *different* ways to implement it, one must find *different* methods of forcing the Polish government to understand that one cannot uproot a mass of millions of people and go unpunished.

Certainly, solving the economic problem of the Jews is much, much more difficult in Poland than in Russia. The Bolsheviks have nationalized all factories, placing them in the hands of government. The Polish government has monopolized the alcohol and tobacco factories and salt mines, and it intends to put its hands on other industries. The Bolsheviks did not compensate the factory owners. I won't start complaining about

---

1 {The Joint Distribution Committee is an American Jewish relief organization founded in 1914. It originally provided assistance to Jews in Ottoman Palestine and later expanded its efforts to Eastern Europe. ORT (*Obshchestvo remeslennogo truda* in Russian, the Association for the Promotion of Skilled Trades, or the Organization for Rehabilitation through Training) was founded in Russia in 1880 to provide vocational training for Jewish youth.}

it here. The Polish government paid the factory owners well—and the Jewish factory owners too. But it chased out all Jewish workers and salaried employees from the monopolized enterprises. Five or six Jewish owners of tobacco factories received fat sums and now run other business with their money, but the several thousand Jewish workers and office workers who worked for decades in these factories, giving up their young years and their lungs in them were rudely and cruelly thrown out on the street. Ostensibly, they were also compensated, but that sufficed only for funeral shrouds, not for making a living.

Jewish workers were employed in the Polish tobacco industry for more than 50 years. For decades they formed the majority in the industry. One may say that the Polish tobacco industry stands on Jewish bones because many hundreds of Jewish workers caught tuberculosis in its factories and died an early death.

Already in 1885 around 1,000 Jewish workers and very few Christians were employed in the tobacco industry in Warsaw. Now in the state tobacco factories there are 1,600 workers but not one Jew. Certainly no fewer than 10,000 workers and office workers are employed in this industry in all of Poland.

Even a few years ago it was a Jewish industry. The office workers were almost all Jews, as was a majority of the manual workers. Now only in Grodno, in the once famous Shereshevski tobacco factory, there remain around 300 Jewish workers. The managers of the factory, among whom there is not one Jew, are driving out the last few Jewish workers. They fire Jews at the least excuse and immediately hire Christian replacements. It is easy to imagine how Jewish workers must feel in such a factory, where they know their days are numbered; where they sense that their bosses are seeking reasons to fire them; where bosses often cause them to feel that they are superfluous. Only inhuman need, only hunger in the most literal sense of the word, forces these few Jewish workers to endure.

This, then, is *national* Bolshevism—expropriating from private owners, like the Bolsheviks, but so that Jewish manual and office workers pay the price for it. The few rich factory owners who received large sums of money from the government quickly find an alternative way to make a living, but what of the several thousand Jewish workers and several hundred Jewish office workers?

However, national Bolshevism does not affect only the Jewish proletarian. It is consistent and goes further. The tobacco industry is government owned and one can no longer deal with it freely. One must have a concession from the government, and in granting concessions the government squeezes the Jews again. For example, in a city like Pinsk, where all 26 tobacco concessions were owned by Jews, 10 were handed over to Christians. And that is in Pinsk, situated close to the Russian border, where there are almost no Poles apart from the officials sent there, and the Byelorussians are almost all country folk who do not yet compete with the Jews in trade or in artisanal work. In that city, Christian shopkeepers were inserted in more than one-third of the tobacco stores that used to be completely in Jewish hands. And in the real Poland, a few concessions are thrown to the Jews but most are given to one's own. Thus Jewish shopkeepers are also ruined.

Salt is also a monopoly in Poland. And in the quintessentially Jewish city of Pinsk, where 98% of storekeepers are Jews, all six concessions are effectively in Christian hands. Jews run five of them, but Christians share in the profits and this will probably last only until the Christians learn the trade, at which point they will show the Jews the door.

And while we are considering Pinsk, let us add a few more facts that will immediately clarify how the Jews are being encircled—especially poor Jews, but also middle-class Jews—and how in a free political republic a Jewish economic ghetto is being created. In Pinsk, as noted earlier, 98% of storekeepers are Jews. And industry too is almost completely in Jewish hands. Not only are the factory owners Jews; a large number of workers are too. Pinsk is a real Jewish city, as will be later elaborated.

In Pinsk a branch of the state bank opened {in the 1920s}. To whom should it offer credit if not to Jewish factory owners, merchants, and storekeepers? It turns out that the bank gives credit only to landowners, even when their estates are burdened with debt, and to Christian cooperatives. If, with great effort, a Jewish cooperative credit association manages to get credit, it is small in comparison with the credit received by the area's Christian-owned cooperatives.

One may assume that the director of the state bank is completely against giving credit to merchants and storekeepers. But there opens in Pinsk a Christian-owned paper business and the owner immediately receives a substantial sum of credit. Yet in Pinsk there is a Jewish-owned paper business that is 65 years old, and the Jew is denied credit so he must get credit from private sources at 25–30% interest, while the Pole borrows money from the state bank at 10–12%. If one adds that the office holder who collects taxes is also a Pole who feels it his obligation and a good national deed to charge the Jew higher and higher taxes and to demand payment with the greatest strictness, one gets a clear picture of how the Jew in the free Polish Republic is surrounded by iron rings that cut into his body, wounding him more seriously than do political constraints.

In the Galician oil fields there were several hundred Jewish workers and many Jewish office workers. Since the founding of the Oil Trust, in which the government is a major shareholder, the number of Jewish workers keeps on falling. It is very close to the time when oil drilling, in which Jews worked hard for decades, will be *Judenrein*. The Oil Trust is also engaged in a war with Jewish oil merchants, who will suffer from it.

Much has been written about liquor concessions and I will not repeat it all here. But here in Poland there is a brand new edict regarding commerce. In the Polish wood trade, the Jews are nearly alone. They are the large wood merchants who export all kinds of lumber. They are the big specialists in felling trees, measuring forests, selecting and sorting lumber, and manufacturing various wood products. The government arrived at the idea that it will no longer sell its forests to private individuals and will cultivate them itself. The government owns 50–60% of all forests in the country. Besides, the government was until now the largest customer of manufactured wooden goods. Thousands of Jewish workers in the forests have been fired and hundreds of small Jewish merchants were left without bread. I had the opportunity to speak with a Jewish lumber merchant. He has four to five thousand dollars, about 40,000 *zloty*, which in Poland is a large amount of capital. Yet in the eyes of this nearly rich man I saw such desperation, such a lost look, that he elicited great pity in me. He gave the best 30 years of his life to the forest, and now, in his early 50s, beginning anew, searching, risking his savings, starting out on a new path, fear grips him. The man lost his courage and belief in himself.

But a thousand times more desperate and terrifying is the situation of the Jewish forest workers, who have not saved even a month's living expenses and who must now seek new occupations. They want to throw themselves into the ocean. They are so forlorn, lost, and beaten down that they can do almost nothing.

Forestry employed some 20–25,000 Jews. Jobs for a few thousand Jewish shopkeepers and a few thousand artisans were generated by their work. Life is interconnected; the livelihoods of the Jewish storekeeper and the Jewish artisan depend ultimately on the Jewish population. When thousands of Jewish manual and office workers in the tobacco industry, thousands of Jewish lumber traders, and hundreds of salt and liquor sellers lose their livelihood, it inevitably has strong repercussions for Jewish storekeepers and artisans.

You know already from telegraphic dispatches that the government is planning to incorporate grain sales in its state office, which will be directly tied to peasants and peasant cooperatives, eliminating all intermediaries from the grain market. This will affect many tens of thousands of Jewish families, so it is no wonder that it has elicited such panic and fear in Jewish society.

Already now the government is issuing permits for exporting grain, but not one Jew is among the 18 people in the government office that allocates the licenses—and it is understandable that Jewish exporters must wait much longer than non-Jews for permits while preference is given to big {non-Jewish} landowners. Jews feel that the grain trade, which directly and indirectly supports half a million Jews, is slipping out of Jewish hands; that flax will soon follow the fate of grain because the government is already talking about organizing the flax trade; that after flax can come another product and yet another, so the Jewish masses are deeply alarmed and find themselves gripped by hysteria. If one adds the general {economic} crisis—which has affected Jews more than others, and which we will consider later—to the aforementioned factors, it becomes evident why the Jews find themselves in such an hysterical, unnaturally nervous, agitated state.

All the mentioned government monopolies are essentially progressive phenomena. If they were just a struggle against the middleman, we could not and would not be permitted to object to them. If they were only such a struggle, they would not disturb the Jews so much. If, when the government took over the tobacco industry, it continued to employ Jewish manual workers and salaried employees, we would have nothing against it. And even in lumber and grain exports, if Jews remained state salaried employees, we would have to greet the state monopolies, even if a certain percentage of Jews would suffer from it. But in Poland, *national Bolshevism* prevails. As soon as a branch of the economy is monopolised it becomes *Judenrein*. It is not just the Jewish factory owner, large lumber merchant or large grain exporter who is ruined, as was the case in Russia, but also the Jewish worker, the Jewish salaried employee, the small Jewish merchant, and the Jewish artisan. The Jewish masses are rudely and cruelly thrown onto the street and it is not even considered necessary to be interested in the question of what will become of these *déclassé* impoverished masses. Here, against national Bolshevism, which wraps itself in a virtuous, socially progressive prayer shawl and causes a Jewish catastrophe, one must mount the greatest struggle.

The question that presents itself is, "Should one struggle against the *national* aspects of these reforms or against the reforms themselves?" We believe the former.

All the misconceptions that claim the government is undertaking these reforms only because of antisemitic blindness and they must inevitably fail economically are self-delusional and will yield no good results. For the first few years, the Polish government will perhaps run the lumber and grain trades worse than the Jews do, but its public servants will eventually learn the necessary skills and perform better than the small-town Jewish agents and buyers. Thus in the Pinsk region, which has much forested land, the Polish government is founding a higher forestry institute and a high school to prepare forestry specialists. And those employees who graduate from the schools will probably understand how to handle lumber so it will not rot no less well than do the Jews who learned it from practice.

We live in a time of regulation and organization, when governments have a great influence on economic life, in a time of trusts and syndicates, of planned economies with defined goals. We are no longer in a position—nor is it in our interest—to turn back the wheel of history. One must also remember that all those states neighbouring Russia must follow it, not because of their love of Bolshevik ideals but because they are forced to do so economically. Here is an example of how Bolshevik Russia forces a neighbouring country to nationalize a branch of industry. In the last year, Poland exported fully 100 million *zloty* of lumber less than in 1928. Why? Because Russia, which needed foreign currency and had no grain to export, sold lumber so cheaply that nobody could compete with her. Specialists told me that Soviet Russia charged only for rail transportation and labour costs, but nothing for the lumber itself. It is likely that this competition from Soviet Russia led the Polish government to the idea of taking over the Polish lumber industry in its entirety. The Polish government must have foreign currency to survive and will probably follow Russia's Soviet government and sell its lumber for a low price.

We cannot resent the Polish government for wanting to organize its purchase of grain from the peasantry so it does not pass through five pairs of hands—all Jewish hands—and goes directly from the peasant to state warehouses and from there to export markets. In this way the peasant will receive higher prices, and one can have nothing against this. But we all have the right to demand that salaried employees in the state warehouses and public servants working in this branch can be Jews. In practice, however, Jews are not allowed in, and the government does not consider it necessary to even do anything for the *déclassé*, impoverished masses whose number keeps on growing.

In the contemporary state—not just among the Bolsheviks but also in all European states—and especially in the newly independent states such as Poland, Lithuania, Latvia, and so on, civil servants occupy a tremendously large place. This class grew quickly everywhere and now makes up a much larger percentage {of the labour force} than it did before the war. Together with the mass of salaried employees and workers in state and municipal enterprises, they form a large part of the population. In Russia, the percentage of Jews among civil servants is large, but Poland tries hard to ensure that Jews will have no place in this class. Not only are Jews excluded from office jobs, but even from unskilled manual labour on the railroads, in state railroad workshops, as railroad porters, street sweepers, road repair workers—everywhere the same system prevails. The Jews must be segregated in their economic ghetto and not permitted any work for the state or the municipality.

Here are just a few statistics from Warsaw. In 1928, the municipal streetcar corporation employed 4,342 manual workers and salaried employees. Of these, two were Jews. The Bundist faction in the city council fought two years for these two positions. In 1929, an additional

1,500 workers and salaried employees were hired, among them only four Jews. And that was at a time when thousands of Jewish workers remained unemployed for years and were prepared to undertake the hardest work just to earn enough for bread.

The shamelessness of the antisemitic Warsaw city hall goes still further. In 1928, 1,857 manual workers and salaried employees were employed in the water and sewage department, among them a few tens of Jews. This year, employment grew by more than a thousand, and all Jews have been fired. Excluding the Jewish hospital, the Jewish home for the elderly, and the Jewish foundling house, the municipal council employed more than 20,000 people, among them about 50 Jews—one-quarter of one percent. Meanwhile, Jews compose one-third of Warsaw's population and contribute more than one-half of all taxes.

And concerning taxes, Jews, neither the living nor the dead, have been at all pitied. This week the following occurred in Warsaw: The tax collector came to a religious Jewish widow demanding six *zloty*. Because she could not pay, he took her featherbed. The widow went out to the courtyard and burst into tears. The neighbours, all poor, collected among themselves six *zloty* and bought back the featherbed from the tax collector. That is how taxes are collected from Jews.

Before me lies a copy of a request from a Jewish woman storekeeper, Brokhe Pshekupnik from Byala, to the tax office in Lublin. This document would be worth showing to the Polish ambassador in Washington, who not long ago boasted before a delegation from the Polish-Jewish Federation that Jews in Poland are living in an actual paradise. Brokhe Pshekupnik writes that various taxes totalling 200 *zloty* are being demanded of her. The tax collector removed from her store 4 kg of rice, 4 kg of kidney beans, 5 kg of cereal, 2 kg of sugar, and 50 lime pellets.[2] The store's entire stock is worth a little more than 13 *zloty*, a dollar and a half, and they are demanding 200 *zloty* from her.

One of the most burdensome statutes, really a pharaonic edict that has the greatest peril for the entire class of Jewish artisans, more than one-third of the Jewish population, is the well-known guild regulation. Special master exams are being instituted, and in practice conditions have been created that will cause Jewish artisans to fail so that young

---

2   {Lime contains nutrients essential for plant growth. It also lowers soil acidity, which increases the availability of nutrients.}

Jewish apprentices will never be able to achieve the title of master. Just the fact that the exams are conducted in Polish by Polish examiners will mean that thousands of older Jewish artisans who know their trade much better than the examiners will fail.

Still worse is the situation with youth. According to the law, every apprentice must, while employed in a workplace, take evening courses in general and special technical subjects. This is a fine law, like those among people in civilized countries. However, for Jews {in Poland} this nice law is really a deadly poison. In all of Poland, 92,000 male and female apprentices are now enrolled. Only 3,000 of them are Jews, around 3%, when Jews make up more one-half of all artisans in Poland. In Warsaw alone, 11,000 young people are enrolled in such courses, only 327 of them Jews—3%.

One might think that Jews do not want to send their children to these courses, but that is not so. Rather, it is made difficult for Jews to send their children to these courses. The courses are purposely conducted only in Christian parts of the city. If a Jewish apprentice manages to take such a course, they hide his hat and his coat, they pour ink on his notebook, they beat him, and they ridicule him when he does not answer questions in fluent Polish. In general, they poison his life so he must flee. For the sake of justice they would need to open separate courses in Yiddish, but in Poland justice is not practicable, so Jews must take care of themselves. {To take such courses} one needs the consent of officials and a lot of money to buy it.

Of course, we have not developed all the points mentioned here. One could write an entire dissertation about each point. About taxes alone once could write a new *"Eykhe"*[3] because one cannot meet in Poland one Jew who does not complain about how taxes are choking him.

One must remember that until today the richest people in Poland are the big landowners who own large estates. All landowners directly provided 64 million *zloty* for the government in 1928, while trade and industry directly provided 350 million *zloty* in taxes. Although agriculture provides the state treasury with only one-sixth of the amount provided by trade and industry, it received loans and support from the state totalling 470 million *zloty* in the same year and at the same time as

---

3 {The first word in the Book of Lamentations, which mourns the destruction of the first temple in Jerusalem by Babylon in 586 BCE.}

the government treated urban occupations like step-children. Therefore, a double injustice is visited on the Jews. The government sucks the marrow from the urban population and gives it to the countryside. It takes much more in taxes from the city than the countryside, and when it comes to loans the countryside is the prime beneficiary. The Jews are, however, very little occupied in agriculture and can therefore benefit little from the favours that are bestowed on the countryside.

All the facts recounted here are not accidents of one or another public servant. They are *typical* phenomena that are repeated from one city to the next and from one small town to the next. They are a natural result of a political *system* that we have given the name, national Bolshevism.

Yes, in Poland national Bolshevism rages in its worst form. It is much crueller than the Bolshevism of the Soviet Union because it singles out Jews economically, constructs a medieval economic wall between them and the non-Jewish population, and erects a social and class ghetto on top of the political one. The Jewish population is singled out economically and is pushed to the backward corners of economic life. It is encircled by iron economic walls that are more fearful than the ghetto walls of medieval times. This explains the panic that is immediately apparent to Polish Jews, the nervous state that is so well known to us from Bolshevik Russia, the uncertainty of the next day. From this derives the fear of sudden, unforeseen actions on the part of office holders for whom the Jew is really like clay in the potter's hands. From this derives the psychology of "better spend the little money one has because they will in any case take it from you" and the psychology that in Poland one can achieve nothing, there looms only sorrow upon sorrow, so whoever can must run away, save himself as soon as possible because later it will be worse.

5. A flood of small promissory notes[1]

A few hours after arriving in Warsaw I went into a café to eat. Here was my first meeting with two "matchmakers" of a completely new type who flung me immediately into the depressed mood that envelops all Polish Jews.

They were two Jews from Kiev. Both were once quite rich. They were ruined a little by pogroms and a lot by the Bolsheviks. In 1920 they ran away from Russia with nothing. One of them lost his wife on the way. She could not overcome the anguish and misery of stealing across the border and took her own life after crossing it.

I first became acquainted with these Jews at the time of the pogroms in Kiev when we sat on duty entire nights waiting for the pogromists in order to sound an alarm over all Kiev, wake up the Jews, and instil fear in the pogromists. Such an acquaintanceship brings people quite close, even if they are from very different classes or camps. They carry in their souls a common secret that connects them forever. I was truly happy to see my old acquaintances.

One glance at them was enough to notice two completely ruined people, lost, dejected, hopeless, candidates for throwing themselves from a fifth-floor window, which is again becoming fashionable in Warsaw, as it was a few years ago. They had already experienced during

---

1 {A promissory note is a form of debt that is incurred in lieu of payment for a good or service. It is a signed commitment by the issuer to pay the provider of the good or service a specified sum on demand or by a certain date. The payment may include interest. A promissory note may be sold at a discount to a third party, who may in turn sell it at a further discount to a fourth party, and so on. The ultimate holder of the promissory note expects to receive payment from the issuer on demand or by a certain date, depending on the terms of the note.}

their nine-year wandering more than one metamorphosis. They had been money changers, manufacturers, and real estate brokers, had tried to enter the market with a little merchandise, and were most recently promissory note "matchmakers."

In Poland one pays everyone for everything with promissory notes, even the doctor and the dentist, who later discount the promissory notes on the street. Eighty percent of Jewish workers are paid with promissory notes. I say "Jewish" because the gentiles with their good gentile heads do not understand such schemes as a 20-*zloty* promissory note ($2.25) which one must take to the stock exchange and sell for 17 *zloty*, or even for 15.

On the other hand, I was told in Bialystok a few years ago that the Jewish factory owners survived the 1924–25 economic crisis thanks to the small-denomination promissory notes that they paid their workers, allowing them to bring capital into circulation that they would have otherwise never obtained. The German factory owners did not rely on such trifles and were all forced to close their factories. When I was in Bialystok a few years ago, all the textile factories were in Jewish hands.

What explains this phenomenon, which probably seems wild and incomprehensible to the reader? Poland lacks capital to run businesses. For a population of 30 million, only 1.5 billion *zloty* are available for businesses while the state budget totals 3 billion *zloty*. There are no loans from abroad. Productivity is just one-sixth that of Germany while the population is one-half as numerous as Germany's. Every *zloty* passes through many hands, and therefore one pays crazy interest rates of 25–30%. Even large firms are often forced to discount promissory notes on the private exchange and pay such high interest rates.

The small promissory note that Jews have often used and often transferred from one person to another has become a sort of second currency in the country—a supplement to the *zloty*. However, it has been reduced to its sickest and most comical form, like paying the teacher, the housemaid, and the doctor with a promissory note. The trade in promissory notes has become so widespread and involved such a large part of the population that a large class of employees has grown up around the business. Some are discounters, people with a little money who can redeem promissory notes {for a sum less than their face value} or are such trustworthy people they can deposit them in a bank. Others are "matchmakers," or brokers as they are called in various cities, who bring together promissory note sellers and buyers.

In small towns, the "Americans"—those who receive $10–15 a month from relatives {abroad}—make a living from buying promissory notes. The big and the small have issued promissory notes, and it is understandable that in such a trade system the mildest breeze can shake the entire structure. A new edict ruins a branch of the economy and bankrupts thousands of Jews. Much mud in the autumn months results in few promissory note redemptions in the small towns and many overdue redemptions. The smallest tremor in the foreign grain market—in general, the smallest movement in one or another wall of the Polish economic structure—gives the entire building such a jolt that all the walls start shaking and cracking, and throughout the country portfolios begin to swell with unredeemable promissory notes. The crisis arrives.

To better understand the paper building made of promissory notes and its role in Jewish life one must add that promissory note redemption is most highly developed in those occupations that are almost completely in Jewish hands and in which this type of trade was already widespread before the war. Even before the war, the norm was that no textile merchant dies before he goes bankrupt a few times. The entire Lodz textile trade, 90% or more of which is in Jewish hands, deals only with promissory notes. The factory owner lends to the big merchant, the big merchant to the wholesaler, and the wholesaler to the storekeeper, who sells for cash, especially to the peasant. Recently, however, the consumer has been taught to write little promissory notes. And the mountain of little promissory notes keeps on growing.

Lodz got wind of an American system that involves paying instalments, in this way making it easier for consumers to buy things they cannot afford to pay for all at once with cash. The consumer has thus been inundated with merchandise. It is enough to be in Poland only briefly to immediately sense that there is too much Jewish energy, too much Jewish entrepreneurial vigour, for the small Polish state. Once, this energy had an outlet: far and wide Russia and also emigration to America. Today it is as if it is shut in a cage, accumulated, concentrated in a limited number of branches that lie in Jewish hands. And this Jewish energy has started cultivating the internal market, forcing it to consume as much cloth as Lodz can produce, creating artificial demand in the population.

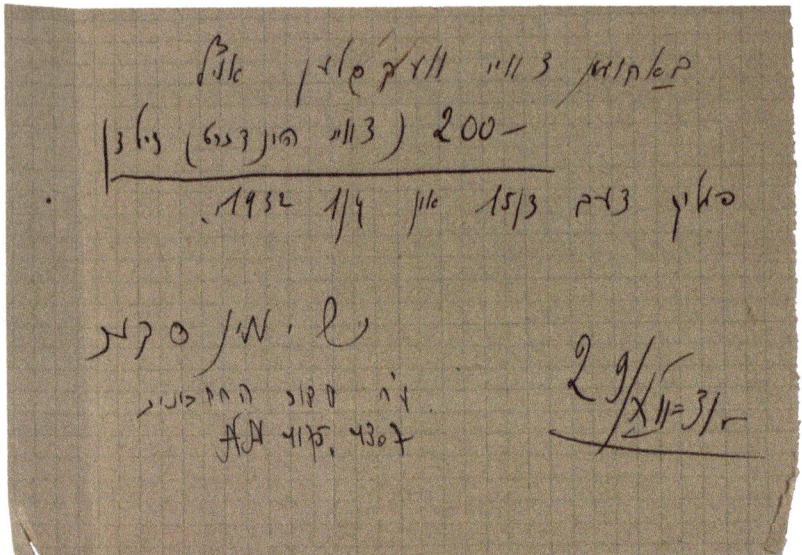

Fig 4 Untitled handwritten note (1931), Vilna, Lithuania. ©Archives of the YIVO Institute for Jewish Research, New York. The note reads: "Received two promissory notes for 200 (two hundred) gildn {*zloty*} due 15 March and 1 April 1932. Sh. Minsker, 29 December 1931." https://archives.cjh.org/repositories/7/archival_objects/1167339

Lodz worked well for a few years, but it received for its merchandise fat portfolios of promissory notes on which there were tens of thousands of signatures. One can pay the Jewish worker with promissory notes but not the Christian worker. Besides, one must purchase raw materials abroad, and for that one must pay cash. A crisis therefore had to happen, though in normal times it would not have been so terrible.

An unfortunate circumstance occurred that suddenly made the crisis a general one in all branches of the economy but mainly in branches where Jews are more highly represented. The price of grain fell so sharply that peasants earned one-half of what they earned a year earlier. Precisely in Poland there was a good harvest this year but low prices in foreign markets resulted in the peasants having just enough to cover the expenses they need to continue farming.

If the peasant has no money, the small-town Jewish storekeeper feels it immediately. The shopkeeper transmits the feeling to the mid-sized storekeeper via unredeemed promissory notes and, as if through an electric current, unredeemed promissory notes convey the sad tidings to the wholesaler and the factory owner. Once the hail of unredeemed promissory notes starts crashing down, it does not stop. Like an epidemic, it spreads to broader and broader circles. Even those who can redeem promissory notes do not want to give up the last bit of cash they own. Much abuse, failure to redeem notes, and making a mockery of those who demand payment ensues. One or two bankruptcies in a small town is a calamity and a disgrace for the bankrupted, but hundreds and thousands of bankruptcies is no longer a disgrace but just a calamity.

A frivolous, even cynical relationship to money obligations in business has developed. This is a result of the mountain of small promissory notes and overdue redemptions under which Jewish business in Poland is being choked.

The Polish nobleman borrows money from the state bank or large private banks—large sums for long terms. In difficult times, he has tens of good friends in the banks, which administer payments for promissory notes. Overdue redemption of promissory notes among these people are rare, lacking a mass character. Heavy industries, which are to a great extent in Polish hands, suffer much less from the crisis.

The coal mines sell abroad or to the state. Only a small percentage of their production generates revenue from local private buyers. The metal factories also work a lot for the state, providing locomotives and railroad cars, or for large factories, providing machines. Unlike most Jewish-owned industry, they do not have to bother with the mass consumer and the mass storekeeper. Overdue redemptions probably occur among them, but they are for large sums and have better prospects of being redeemed than do the hundreds of thousands of small Jewish promissory notes for insignificant sums. One can confidently accept that the great majority of overdue promissory notes are Jewish-owned.

I have spent so much time discussing the promissory note and overdue redemption epidemic because it reveals most plainly the sickliness and abnormality of Jewish economic life in Poland. When the abscess bursts it will certainly have a colossal impact on the fate of the Jews in Poland.

The whole time, the Polish government follows a policy in which "Polish industry" receives immeasurably more credit than so-called "Jewish industry." It continually complains that there are too many middlemen in Poland, making Polish merchandise expensive. Now it will have enough evidence that this is indeed the case and will certainly take steps to regulate trade in a way that Jews will lose their livelihoods.

We do not deny that there are too many small Jewish storekeepers. However, we demand that the state should not only want fewer middlemen, but also that they should be able to find livelihoods in other economic domains. The government will nonetheless act as always: taking livelihoods from Jews but not finding them new ones.

Apart from the government there are additional important factors that will and must cause thousands and perhaps hundreds of thousands of Jews to emerge from the present crisis without bread and without hope for bread:

- Large factory owners and large, solid merchants who have considerable sums of capital have decided to reorganize the sale of merchandise so that the wholesaler will be eliminated. They try to create direct ties to individual storekeepers, small storekeepers, and even village storekeepers.

- Whoever is familiar with the condition of Jewish trade in Poland knows that, precisely among middling wholesalers, Jews are the strongest element, while among individual storekeepers, who have to deal directly with the Christian masses, Polish storekeepers have won significant victories in competition with the Jews.

- In the current crisis it turns out that the Jewish middling storekeeper owns almost none of his own capital and works only with borrowed merchandise and money. For the factory owner or large merchant it has thus became clear that it is much less risky to lend to the small storekeeper, and it is also better insofar as it will make merchandise less expensive. One must remember that in Poland the factory owner's merchandise usually passes through four or five hands before reaching the consumer, making merchandise expensive.

For these reasons, in the next few years many victims from the Jewish middleman classes will fall—in addition to those who have already fallen so heavily that they will not be able to revive even after the crisis.

We have left behind the "matchmakers" and acquainted the reader with the mountain of ash that became of the hundreds of thousands of small promissory notes, each of which passed through tens of Jewish hands and created among the Jews a fantastic conception of real trade and real profit that, like ash, comes to nothing when a slight breeze blows. The two "matchmakers" painted for us such a vivid picture of the mountain of ash that Jews had scaled for years, believing that they were making the world turn when in fact they were just fooling themselves, that I trembled with fear. As long as the wheel turned, Jews turned with it, intoxicated and enchanted by the easy dealings of trade with little papers. Suddenly a spoke broke. The wheel stopped, and all the enchantment was gone with the wind.

After the first overdue redemptions and bankruptcies, additional lending ceased. Since it was not possible to receive merchandise on loan, it was not worthwhile to pay for merchandise received earlier because one would wind up with empty shelves. Bankruptcies spread. Factories increasingly refrained from providing merchandise in exchange for promissory notes. Bankruptcies then multiplied, and fear of lending merchandise grew still stronger. Thus did people drag one another into the abyss, creating a mood of despair, panic, and desperation that strengthened the crisis still more, dragging into the abyss those who had previously stood on sufficiently firm ground. The wheel stopped, and after all their frenetic dealings, Jews became convinced that all was lost when they saw that one was left with worthless promissory notes, another with empty shelves. Getting the wheel to turn again was impossible without radical reforms that would require many victims.

I left the promissory note "matchmakers" who, for almost a month, had not earned a penny, and moved on to Genshe Street,[2] the centre of the Jewish textile trade, a narrow, dirty, and always noisy little street that before the war had so many millionaires—real, solid, well-established millionaires. It is still now the richest little street in the Jewish quarter, but how much it and its representatives have changed!

Gone are the large firms that sold textiles in the Moscow region. Of the several hundred firms that I counted with a representative of a firm that was established 35 years ago, just nine existed before the war. All the rest were established after the war and were based on wartime and post-war speculation, inflation trickery, and military supply contracts.

---

2 {Now Anielewicz Street.}

They were owned by upstarts and also people full of bombast, among whom one cannot know whether they are really rich men or only painted in the colours of rich men. Among them one often discovers that the father of the family jumped from a fifth story window and in this manner extricated himself from the complications of writing and receiving promissory notes, while his family members were enjoying themselves somewhere abroad in the best and most expensive spa.

Hundreds of old, solid, secure, firms have gone under. Many of their owners ran to Russia, where they ended their days as beggars or in a poor house. Many met the same fate in Warsaw, and in their last years dragged themselves down the same Genshe Street, ragged and tattered, unrecognized by their own former salesclerks, their heirs. This is a very interesting page of Jewish war history that must still be written.

One thing is clear. In recent years, the composition of the Jewish trade bourgeoisie has completely changed. In 90% of cases, we have before us an entirely new class, composed of previous salesclerks and office workers of bankrupted firms where they used to work. They lack the traditions and ambitions of the old firms and follow the principle of grabbing whatever you can and as much as you can because God alone knows what tomorrow may bring. This new post-war "morality" in the world of trade creates the most fitting atmosphere for the relaxed underwriting of little promissory notes, the acceptance of high interest rates, selling merchandise below cost in order to receive cash, and not taking to heart one's failure to honour the terms of promissory notes.

I sat with my acquaintance in his business at around six o'clock in the evening. Before the war, he had 22 employees, now only five. But there was nothing to do. They don't sell for promissory notes and no customers buy for cash. I saw the same situation in a few businesses that I visited.

Of course, among the newly founded firms there are also reliable, serious undertakings that actually have their own capital—but they are in the minority.

On the way I dropped in to a watchmaker, ostensibly to fix my watch. Before me sat a hunchbacked Jew with sunken cheeks and dulled eyes who appeared to be between 55 and 58 years old. He was reading a newspaper. From my conversation with him I learned that he was only 45 years old, that he had earned nothing for the last three days, but that he could not deny himself a newspaper because otherwise he would go mad thinking about how to make a living and not coming up with anything. So he borrows a newspaper from the newspaper vendor. His children are in Russia, but he has no letters from them and he does not know whether they are alive. He ended: "One lives alone in need and in poverty, without consolation and without hope, and one begs for the Angel of Death, who refuses to come out of spite."

After visiting the depressed watchmaker I left for the headquarters of the Jewish trade unions. On the way I passed a street that was completely occupied by hat businesses and workshops. I knew the street well because I had lived there before the war. Besides that, I often visited the shops on the street with my relatives, who came from my hometown to Warsaw to buy merchandise.

The businesses were always swarming with customers. The provincial buyers used to have to wait for a long time before they were shown product. In the Warsaw tradition, a shop was small and narrow. Deep in the courtyard was its workshop, where ten or so young women worked. In the shop itself, the owners, their daughter or son, and a few non-family female employees served customers. The employees helped each customer select appropriate fashions. The young salesclerks already knew the taste of buyers from each Russian area. A Jew from Minsk received completely different merchandise than a Jew from Kherson.

Crowded into this kind of shop would be ten or so Jewish provincial buyers from Lithuania, Poland, White Russia, Ukraine, the Caucasus, and so on. There was a mishmash of dialects and tones, temperaments and characters. I used to often think that here is a splendid laboratory for scholarly Jews and philologists to study the variety of Yiddish types and pronunciations. Customers would remain in the shop until late at night, often with the doors and shutters closed. Customers would be let in and out through the door.

I was especially curious to see how the once-teeming street now appeared, so I visited it about five times, at various times of day. I always saw one or two young Jewish women standing perfectly still for a long time by the glass doors of the shops. Their eyes were straining, as if looking for someone, waiting and never seeing what they are waiting for. On their faces, dull and tired from doing nothing, the entire sorrow of the starved street was etched.

Here I sensed in its entirety the tragedy of the thousands and tens of thousands of Jews who had been employed in and around Jewish small industry, which worked for great Russia and is now cut off from that market. In the sorrow of the eyes of these few tens of young women, standing entire days leaning on the glass doors of the street's shops and looking out for someone who does not come, here for 15 years one can read the entire extent of the tragedy of thousands of Jewish workers and employees. They have lost their work and their trades, so they seek new sources of income but find nothing, and they discover also that the doors of all countries are barred and sealed to them.

One feels this even more in the emigration office. There I met 30 people, all workers or artisans. Not one storekeeper or merchant was among them—not because the latter do not need to emigrate, but because it is more difficult for them to obtain a visa and more frightening form them to leave their place. There is now absolutely no doubt that Jewish merchants, especially the small ones, are in a much sadder situation than artisans and workers. They certainly comprise a large percentage of emigrants, but first they or their children undergo a process of "productivisation." That is, they earlier learned a trade and afterwards resolve to leave for a foreign country. They are ready to travel to any far corner of the world just to escape. They are ready to risk their lives, the quicker to transport themselves across the border. Sadly, however, the possibilities are tragically few.

Still, hundreds of people come to the emigration office and leave despondent: here is a quota and there one needs an invitation from relatives. Here one must be a farmer and there one must have a mountain of money—600 or 700 dollars—when disembarking from the ship. Some 20–25,000 Jews are now leaving Poland annually, about one-quarter of the total emigration from Poland, where Jews make up 10% of the population. But this is a drop in the ocean, a minimal number that can ease the situation of Jews in Poland very little.

6. Jews are collapsing in the streets from hunger

> I have no mother!
> I have no father!
> I'm hungry!
> I'm barefoot!
> Jews! Give me work!
> Jews! Give me work!

In a Warsaw courtyard that looked like a narrow box with high walls, a tall young man stood on spindly legs, his skinny arms hanging by his sides, and shouted—shouted as if he were tearing out pieces of his innards and hurling them at the high, deaf stone walls. He grew tired, rested a few seconds, caught his breath, extended his thin neck, and again cried from the depths of his sunken stomach:

> I have no mother!
> I have no father!
> I'm hungry!
> I'm barefoot!
> Jews! Jews! Give me work!
> Jews! Spare me some change!
> Have pity!! Have pity!!

For several minutes he shouted to the deaf walls of the narrow box, and nobody responded.

I accompanied the young man along the street for a while, unable to tear myself away from him. To this day his visceral cries haunt me. To this day I see his burning, agitated eyes. This thin, withered figure, these desperate cries without impact and without conviction that there might be any response, this exhausted, weakened face with its two agitated sockets seemingly searching through darkness—this image has subconsciously developed in my eyes into the symbolic figure of Polish Jewry.

I have just spent five days in Warsaw. Of these, three were during the Lemberg pogrom.[1] In Warsaw they beat Jewish students at the university and technical school. In the streets one could feel the tense psychological state of Jews awaiting a pogrom. The first pages of the newspapers described how waves of pogroms were flooding the streets of Krakow, Czestochowa, Vilna, and Lublin and threatening to flood the whole of Poland. Jews grew quieter, anxiously focused, and apparently *ashamed*. Ashamed of their own weakness, helplessness, and exhaustion; ashamed of their absurd fate of forever being brutalized…

Fig. 5 *A woman sitting next to a corpse in the street* (undated), Lvov, Poland. ©Yad Vashem Photo Archive, Jerusalem, https://photos.yadvashem.org/photo-details.html?language=en&item_id=100293&ind=66

I have been to Poland several times in recent years and seen with my own eyes how three million Jews are being suffocated, but never before had I been seized by such sadness, such grief. Never before did I experience such a depression, such an urge to run through the streets of Jewish

---

[1] {On the evening of 26 November 1932, students from the local Lviv Academy of Veterinary Medicine got into a fight with Jews at a café. A Polish student was injured and died, precipitating widespread anti-Jewish rioting by students.}

cities all around the world shouting, "Help! Save them!" It was not just because I was there during the pogrom. Even before the pogrom, as I wandered aimlessly around the Jewish streets, I gazed into the worried faces of the bustling, Jews with long caftans. I encountered the beards of two elderly Jews hitched to a wagon of coal, hunched over as they dragged the heavy wagon along. I met the yearning eyes of the helpless, abandoned youth. Even before the pogrom, the streets of Warsaw plunged me into a dark depression from which I cannot free myself to this day.

Is this just my own personal impression? Perhaps my soul is ill and I see pitch blackness, despair, and helplessness where there is only everyday poverty, as exists among all nations? Alas, it is not so. Alas, my soul is not ill and I would much rather have seen rays of light and hopeful faces—but I did not encounter any. I searched but could not find them.

Let us take a look at some facts in order to understand the situation of Polish Jewry and get a sense of its tragic grief.

"In the gateway of the house at 3 Twarda Street, the porter Borekh Shtikgold suddenly collapsed. The doctor from the first aid service called to the scene established that the cause of Shtikgold's loss of consciousness was exhaustion due to hunger" (*Haynt* [*Today*], 6 October 1932).

"Thirty-seven-year-old unemployed mechanic Yankev Bornshteyn passed out from hunger on Sunday afternoon. He was revived and escorted to the third precinct" (*Folks-tsaytung* [*People's Newspaper*], 4 July 1932).

"Herman Zelmanovitsh, unemployed, is a frequent visitor to the first aid service. He is regularly found unconscious from hunger on the street. On Sunday afternoon, Zelmanovitsh was found lying passed out from hunger on Kopernika Street" (*Folks-tsaytung* [*People's Newspaper*], 4 July 1932).

These kinds of things happen in Warsaw, Lodz, Vilna, Lemberg, and tens of other Polish cities every day. Of course, for every person who collapses on the street, there are dozens who are no less hungry but bear the hunger more easily, hundreds who are three-quarters as hungry, and tens of thousands who do not have enough to eat, who are growing thin and withering away, and who will establish a generation barely capable of work. Someone who collapses on the street gets noticed and registered. Those fasting in silence or wasting away at home do not. However, one only has to wander around the Jewish quarter of Warsaw for a little while to recognize in the pale faces and extinguished eyes hundreds of candidates for collapsing from hunger, thousands of candidates who are truly desperate for a piece of bread.

Over the two years since I had last visited Warsaw, the face of the Jewish quarter had changed dramatically. The people had grown paler, gloomier, shabbier, thinner, more feeble. This state of enfeeblement is undoubtedly the defining characteristic of Polish Jewry. It is feeble not only in the physical sense of the word, but also in the spiritual sense: abandoned, without a father or a mother, without movements to captivate the masses and give them courage and faith in a better future, without great central leaders to comfort them, without central institutions to which they might direct their cry in a time of trouble. Disorganized, torn apart, despondent, and feeble. We will return to this tragedy of fatherless and motherless Polish Jewry later. First, we will consider some additional facts that demonstrate the state of Polish Jewry.

We have seen how people are collapsing in the streets, a phenomenon that we have not read about in the newspapers of any other nation, despite the fact that there are 30 million unemployed people in the world. The suicides among Polish Jews are also highly unusual. Here are several examples:

"Lemberg. A horrible incident took place in the Jewish quarter on the evening of Yom Kippur. Fifty-year-old Berta Grinboym (3 Reja Street) got dressed, took a prayer book, said goodbye to the members of her household, wished them a good year, and then, instead of going to the synagogue, went out onto the balcony and threw herself off. She is in the hospital with no hope of survival. The cause of her suicide was the severe material hardship she was experiencing" (*Haynt* [*Today*], 12 October 1932).

A devout Jewish woman, with a prayer book in her hands, *on the evening of Yom Kippur*—how poisoned must the atmosphere be, how sick the soul of Polish Jewry, how desperate and enfeebled the whole environment, when a person like this throws herself off a balcony at a moment like this.

Here are some additional facts:

"Vilna. The Jewish court intern Shmuel Katsev has committed suicide. The cause was Katsev's removal from court under the suspicion of anti-government activity. He was arrested. The suspicion turned out to be false, but the court would no longer employ him" (*Frimorgn* [*Morning*], 1932, No. 258).

Thus, a young man who has graduated from the juridical faculty and is preparing to become a lawyer is suspected of communism and arrested. This does not seem sufficient to plunge someone into despair. It turns out that the suspicion was unfounded, but this is Poland; a single percentage point of suspicion is enough to block your path to a career. Even without a shred of suspicion, they are still prepared to pile mountains of stones on the path of a Jewish intellectual, and all the more so when you are marred by the taint of political opposition. The young man is removed from court—so he ends his life! Where are the youthful strength, ambitions, obstinacy, and hopes? Where is the feeling of spite that plays such a major role among youth? Where is the hatred and loathing and fury towards the enemy piling stones on your path? All of these things usually give life a sense of purpose, generate wings and energy and spur someone forward to live, to work, to influence, and to fight, but the soul of the Jewish young man in Poland is a desert. His mind is desolate and vacant and his whole being is poisoned. In a feeble mental state, he drags himself and his burden around, and at the first difficult trial, he hands his ticket to the Lord and flees the world.

To understand the psychology of this young Jewish suicide, one must consider the situation of the Jewish intellectual in Poland, as well as that of the Jewish youth in general. Here, a Jewish young man tells of the seven circles of hell he went through as he took his first strides in life. He is studying at a technical school in Warsaw. He is, of course, put through a great deal of misery by his Polish colleagues. He is not only boycotted but also verbally abused, and sometimes worse. From the professors, too, he often hears that Jews should stick to trade and not study technical professions. He bites his tongue, ignores all the insults, and studies. Before graduating, students are required to work for two months in a factory; otherwise, they are not permitted to take the diploma exam. The director has forgotten about the Jewish student and he is left without a work placement. The young Jewish man runs back and forth between the director and the manager and finally gets the director to call the state automobile factory, where they agree to accept a trainee.

The young Jewish man is delighted and the following morning runs happily to the factory. He is received very pleasantly and given a questionnaire to fill out. He completes it honestly with his Jewish name and Jewish faith. The secretary takes the sheet, reads it through—and his whole attitude shifts immediately. He is suddenly as cold as ice; he needs to speak to the factory director, so the young man will have to come back tomorrow. The next day, the gatekeeper will not even let him in. He runs back to the technical school and requests, demands, argues. The director responds that the factory does not want any Jews and there is nothing he can do about it. He cannot get into an argument with the factory's director for the sake of a Jewish student. But the student is unable to complete the exam without the work experience. Using his contacts, he eventually manages to get a placement in the municipal bus workshop and writes the exam.

Dozens of Polish students who wrote the exam at the same time as the Jewish man get jobs right away. Meanwhile, he takes his diploma and knocks on door after door, getting rejected each time. After many months of running around, and through a great number of connections and requests, he manages to get hired in the streetcar workshops as an *unskilled labourer*. He is prepared to do anything just to have a job, to end his idleness, to start earning something. He needs a certificate from a municipal doctor showing that he is healthy. On the certificate, the doctor lists illnesses that the young man has never even heard of. The engineering graduate is back on the street, without work and without any hope of finding a place for himself. He is later hired in those same streetcar workshops for *temporary* work. He has the necessary physical strength, but where can he find the courage not to lose faith in himself and throw himself off the fifth-floor balcony?

We have recounted this story in great detail because it is a typical everyday occurrence. This is the fate of the entire Jewish intelligentsia in Poland—and not just the intelligentsia.

Here is a set of truly shocking facts:

The Rovne city hall reduced its number of officials. Of 20 Jewish officials, 14 were fired, more than two-thirds. Of 192 non-Jews, 40 were fired, just a fifth. Jews make up 75% of Rovne's population. Previously, they made up 9% of city hall officials, after the dismissals, fewer than 4%.

The Otvotsk city hall fired almost all Jewish officials, even though they hired several new non-Jewish ones.

In the Grodno municipal tobacco factory—formerly the Shereshevski factory, where hundreds of Jews had sacrificed their health over dozens of years—they promptly smoked out all the Jews. They recently dismissed 12 Jewish mechanics, several of whom had worked in the factory for more than 30 years. After a great deal of hustling on the part of a representative from the bureau for the right to work and many requests and complaints to the management, they got them to rehire one Jewish mechanic, a 54-year-old man, but only for unskilled labour, not as a tradesman.

On the topic of tobacco, it is worth adding the following. Before the tobacco monopoly was introduced in Poland, the tobacco trade was almost entirely in Jewish hands, with 800 Jewish wholesale businesses. Once the monopoly was introduced, it became necessary to obtain permits to deal in tobacco. Jews were given virtually no permits; of 800 Jewish wholesalers, hardly 30 remained. Recently, they took away the permits of these 30 as well, and thus tore from the Jews a branch of economic life that had formerly been exclusively Jewish; the tobacco manufacturers, tobacco workers, tobacco employees, and tobacco dealers had all been Jews. Now barely a trace remains—the state has taken over the entire branch, and Jews are not allowed to benefit from the state.

Jews must pay taxes, license fees, and various other contributions to the state, but they are forbidden from benefitting from it. Not only are they barred from jobs in the administration, the official apparatus running the state, but they are also prevented from working in the state factories, sweeping the municipal streets, and serving as railroad porters. This *hunger principle* with respect to three million Jews is being carried out more consistently, mercilessly, and thoroughly than any other state principle. Compromise is acceptable when it comes to many issues, but not when it comes to giving Jews a livelihood, not when it comes to loosening the rope around the Jews' throats, not when it comes to allowing the tiniest hope to arise in the Jews' hearts that they may one day have equal rights.

Equal rights. The Polish government promptly pulls out the constitution and unfurls it before the world, pointing to where it states clearly and simply that all citizens are equal. Jews are indeed citizens like all others—just not when it comes to carrying baggage on trains, working in a state tobacco factory, measuring and chopping wood in a state forest, selling state sugar, tobacco, salt, or crude oil, and certainly not when it comes to collecting taxes from the population, when it comes to teaching children, even Jewish children in state schools. In sum, one trifling little thing has been taken away from the Jews—a living—and now they are crying out, and collapsing in the streets, and throwing themselves off their top floors in order to break every bone in their bodies, and falling into a depression that screams from tens of thousands of faces on every street in every city of reconstituted Poland.

The Polish government can boast that it has put an end to antisemitism on the streets; they are no longer pulling out beards and *peyes* or throwing Jews out of railroad cars. The current government has one other great merit. A Jew can make a complaint in the dozens of administrative offices and they will hear him out, receiving him politely with a kindly "hello" and a warm "goodbye." Here, however, lies the current regime's cynicism. They lead the Jew to the gallows with a smile on their face and tighten the rope around his neck while acting as though they have invited him to a dance.

After all, what could be more cynical than firing Jewish teachers from schools attended exclusively by Jewish children? What could be more cynical and more merciless than complaining that Jews are too involved in trade while at the same time creating a network of laws meant to suffocate the Jewish artisan and doing everything possible to prevent the emergence of a new generation of Jewish craft workers?

Let us consider one example. The Polish budget allocated more than 20 million *zloty* to professional education. Of that, less than 100,000 *zloty* went to Jewish professional schools, less than 0.5%. This despite the fact that Jews comprise more than one-half of all artisans in Poland and that at least one-half of the license taxes, which are specifically allocated to professional education, are paid out of Jewish pockets.

Every representative of the Republic of Poland in every city of the world shouts that the constitution gives Jews full rights--and they are not lying! One brilliant Polish ambassador in London, a city where Jews really do have equal rights, even had the audacity to claim that the Polish government cannot let things get any better for the Polish Jews, or else Jews from every corner of the world would come rushing to Poland.

Jews in Poland have equal rights—a holy truth, written in the holy constitution, enacted in a holy moment in the life of the Polish nation, the moment when it was liberated from its oppressive yoke after 150 years. Then along came 350 Jews and 150 Christians to take the medical faculty examinations. Out of 150 Christians, 100 passed (two-thirds) and out of 350 Jews, 20 passed (less than 6%). At the dental institute, 350 Jews and 200 Christians took the exam. Out of 200 Christians, 96 passed (48%) and out of 350 Jews, just 18 (5%). Of course, the Polish government cannot be blamed for this. After all, Jews have full rights. If they are blockheads and fail the exams, it must be their own fault...

If we add to all of this the following letter from a Jewish student, it will become entirely clear why Polish Jews are so discouraged, depressed, and enfeebled: "Several days ago, when I was walking along the street with a woman, my student cap was hurled into the mud and I was slapped shamefully for no reason other than because I am a Jew. I am around 30 years old, but that unforgettable evening was the first time that I have felt that I am a Jew, a Jew who hates Poland and Polishness, a beast who wants revenge."

This letter was printed in a Polish weekly. The author of the letter goes on to say how he volunteered as a boy in the Polish army and fought the Bolsheviks for his Polish fatherland in 1920. He was a fierce Polish patriot because he had been raised in a completely assimilated family where he had not been shown a single letter of the Jewish alphabet. As if to spite him, this Polish patriot has an ugly Jewish nose, as he himself expresses it, and on the streets of liberated Poland's capital he was reminded that he is one of the patriarch Abraham's grandchildren.

How many of these Polish patriots with ugly Jewish noses have in recent years in liberated Poland's universities been reminded with clubs and knives that they are Jews! And here we arrive at the incidents in Lemberg. What can we learn from these incidents?

First, that the broad masses of the Polish nation—not to mention the workers—remain indifferent to calls for pogroms. This is certainly a great comfort, a great consolation. I am not trying to fool myself; I am well aware of how deep the antisemitic poison lies within the Polish masses, and the Polish socialists are unpardonable for doing nothing to enlighten the masses or to eradicate the antisemitic venom. On the contrary, with their tactic of keeping themselves at arm's length from the Jewish workers' movement and their fear of advocating openly and more frequently for truly equal rights for Jews, they have stoked antisemitism among the working masses. They are allowing a snake to grow that will eventually repay the Polish socialists with its venom for their sins. Nonetheless, facts are facts: both last year and this one, when the academic hooligans—sons of landowners, manufacturers, clergymen,[2] and high-level officials—were running around with clubs and knives looking for Jewish heads to split open and calling on the masses to take revenge on the Jews, the hungry and desperate masses stayed calm and did not lend a hand in this thuggish patriotic work. This demonstrates that the Polish masses are at a much higher political level than in Ukraine and White Russia, where there have always been enough volunteers to rob and beat Jews.

Second, the recent incidents in Lemberg teach us that the regime explicitly *wanted* a pogrom against Jews. The *Forverts* was entirely correct when it wrote during the pogrom that, if the communists had tried to start a demonstration, or if the Ukrainians had had the audacity to carry a few national flags through the streets of Lemberg, the Lemberg police would have been strong enough and determined enough to immediately shut down such anti-patriotic displays. It turns out that beating a few hundred Jews is not an anti-patriotic enough display for the police to promptly mobilise all their forces. Holes in the heads of a few hundred Jews are not enough of a danger to the fatherland for someone to start shooting, or at least firing cold water from fire hoses, at the knife- and club-wielding patriots.

Everyone in Lemberg is convinced that sending out the fire fighters to blast a stream of cold water at the several hundred student hooligans

---

2 {According to the 1931 census, 15% of Poland's population was non-Catholic and non-Jewish. The great majority of the 15% were Eastern Orthodox. Eastern Orthodox clergymen could have wives if they married before ordination.}

would have been enough to extinguish the pogrom fire. Jewish delegations ran to the governor three times a day, telling him terrible things, bringing facts about hundreds of wounded Jews, yet the head of the city remained unmoved, each time emphasizing that, after all, a Pole had been killed, and for that reason, for that reason....The conclusion was clear: they had to allow the landowners' and clergymen's sons to take revenge for their colleague who was killed in a fight over a prostitute. They had to allow them to live it up and get their fill of Jewish blood.

Why did they have to allow this? There are various explanations. Some say that even in the Warsaw inner circles they thought that the students should be allowed to let off some steam. That way they would have less energy to fight against the government. Others maintain that the governor himself has tight connections to the student hooligans and their families, so he went soft on the students to avoid taking a stand against his own kith and kin.

Whatever the case, pogroms are happening in liberated Poland. They are unlike the ones in Tsarist Russia, but they are still pogroms with hundreds of people wounded.

And what did the Jews do? There is consolation to be found in this regard as well: in the Jewish quarter of Lemberg, things were calm! Why? Because the landowners' sons were simply scared to enter the Jewish quarter, where Jewish porters, butchers, and other workers would have lain into them until they wished they had stayed away. A great comfort! A consolation that invigorates us, makes our blood run faster in our veins, and fills our hearts with indescribable joy. The majority of victims were by themselves on streets where Jews are a minority when they were caught and beaten up.

The educated hooligans' fear of the Jewish porters and butchers is certainly a great consolation. But what did the Jewish population do to assert themselves in an *organized* manner? What was their organized protest and fight against the hooligans? *Nothing!* Absolutely nothing! Unless we count the delegations that went running to the governor a few times a day. Back in Tsarist Russia, we were used to bourgeois Jewish delegations running to the governors, pleading for mercy and demanding justice. However, alongside these mercy-pleaders and justice-demanders, there would be other forces, other powers, who spoke the worthier language of revolvers and bombs.

The excuses that a Jewish self-defence organization would provoke the non-Jewish population even further, that it would help the government spin the whole pogrom as an anti-Christian pogrom led by Jews—both of these excuses were always heard in Russia too. These arguments might be right. A Jewish self-defence organization might lead to more Jewish victims than hiding in cellars and attics. Jewish revolvers certainly cost us a great deal, and yet, they did not refuse to make these sacrifices! They understood that these sacrifices were balm for the Jewish soul, that they were the only morally worthy and nationally acceptable response to pogroms!

The self-defence organizations used to emerge *spontaneously*; they were not the result of cold calculations and sober planning, but spontaneous eruptions of the masses, led and organized by the revolutionary parties. Now, both the mass eruptions and the revolutionary parties are missing. This is because Polish Jewry is weakened, dejected, despondent, disorganized, and exhausted. Of course, a distinction must be made between the Jewish working class and the Jewish *bourgeoisie*; among the former, a spark is still glowing, a candle still flickering, but the general despondence and dejection are extinguishing this spark too, smothering the courage of the working class.

The picture I have sketched is very dark, bleak, and hopeless, but God knows that is not my fault; a mirror can only show what is placed in front of it. Contemplating the political conflagration encircling a large portion of Polish Jewry will make one's heart sink even further. We are referring to the fire that has engulfed eastern Galicia, Volhynia, and the Minsk-Vilna region. Yes, in that area there is a genuine conflagration, and no matter how many hundreds more peasants they shoot, how many dozens more villages they destroy, they will not extinguish the national fire of the Ukrainians and White Russians. They are only fanning the flames and there will inevitably come a moment when the fight will assume the form of open war and open uprisings. Rivers of Polish, Ukrainian, White Russian, and Russian blood will flow and everyone will know why. It is also guaranteed that Jewish blood will flow more than anyone else's, although nobody will know why. Jewish blood will be spilled from all sides, because nobody is with the Jews and everybody is against them.

I cannot elaborate here on this national entanglement that has emerged on the aforementioned national borders. I must simply add that it is a tragic irony of fate that Jews, the most neglected stepchildren of the new Republic of Poland, the stepchildren who are persecuted, tormented, and flogged with every whip that Poland has to offer, are the bearers of Polish culture in the Ukrainian and White Russian regions. They are thus digging their own graves, fanning the flames of hatred against themselves, with inevitably fatal, terribly bloody results.

Jews in the eastern Polish regions are isolated from Polish society of all classes and political leanings. There is not a single Polish party or political movement that maintains close contact with any class of Jews whatsoever, leaving Jews feeling orphaned and neglected. In the Ukrainian and White Russian regions, Jews are surrounded by agitated masses who will eventually burst out of their cages and settle their accounts with their tormenters and persecutors—masses who consider Jews to be messengers and agents of these tormenters and persecutors.

This is the atmosphere in which three million Polish Jews are living. This is the tragedy of Polish Jewry's social position in the surrounding society, the desperation of its psychological state. It is therefore no surprise that they walk from one courtyard to the next crying:

> I have no mother!
> I have no father!
> I'm hungry!
> I'm barefoot!

7. At night in the old market[1]

It is glaringly apparent to everyone who visits Poland that a frightful panic has spread among the Jews of that country. It is not a momentary, day- or month-long panic elicited by temporary, stormy circumstances that is therefore normal in a certain sense. It is a permanent, resident panic that grips the soul of the masses and dominates it for years, a panic that drives one to disbelief in one's own powers, actions and undertakings, in tomorrow, in a future that is even a little better. A sort of nervous agitation is also glaringly apparent in the psychology of the Jewish masses, reminding one of a pogrom atmosphere, a situation from which one must save oneself by fleeing and rescuing whatever and as much as one can. In particular, there is no time and too little goodwill to work out a collective plan publicly and seek a way out. Therefore, everyone does for himself what he can and as much as he can.

Understandably, every Jewish individual is preoccupied. He runs to work in the workshop or the factory, seeks customers to buy his goods, carries a 40-pound box on his shoulders or, dripping sweat, pulls a wagonload of coal, stands in a store and looks out at a potential customer or pursues a charitable, interest-free loan to pay off a promissory note or pay taxes, hangs around the stock exchange or stands in the bank requesting a loan in order to purchase a permit. The individual becomes too strongly devoted to necessity and the social machine, in which he is no more than a than a small wheel, to allow himself to pause and glance into his own soul and get hold of the worm of doubt that eats at his powers and his belief in the success of all his hustling. But the person who understands well the Jewish-Polish masses soon senses that

---

[1] {Leshchinsky published an earlier version of this chapter in 1931, titling it "By Day in the Old Market." The changed title reflects the deteriorating circumstances and Leshchinsky's darkened mood. Leshchinsky, *Di ekonomishe lage*..., op. cit., 63–70.}

the hustle is without an inner fire, without wings, more an externally imposed impetus than the pursuit of a definite goal, more mechanical haste than a sure-footed advance along a defined path.

The rush of the Jewish masses on Nalewki Street[2] in today's Warsaw gives the impression of the convulsions of people who are drowning, of people who sway and plod and spin around in one place. No special rhythm has ever existed in the chaotic hubbub of Jewish Nalewki—it is an inhuman jostling that makes it impossible to move left or right, a jam-packed, black mass of bodies that knock against each other and push each other and yet somehow seem not to move from their place. In contrast, before the war one felt a tempo, a momentum, a fluid energy, a streaming force in this cloud of black kaftans. It extended people from one end of Nalewki to the other, flooded all the side streets and led masses of people into the long, narrow courtyards, from which they disappeared into the cellars, holes and attics, crawling out of them loaded down with mountainous packages or two or three stories of boxes on their shoulders, only to tear once again into the thick, dark cloud, tearing it up and pushing it open, forcing it to split apart and make way for them. And with their heavily loaded shoulders these delivery people shouted out and let everyone know that there, in the narrow, dark courtyards, in the cellars and in the attics, heavy toil was taking place, and products for far and wide Russia were being made by human sweat. Now it is also black on Nalewki and still cramped and impossible to turn around, but there is no life—instead of a mobile mass there is a standing bog, and if one falls in one is stuck, unable to crawl out.

Before we seek to clarify these reasons, we will sketch a few pictures torn out of real life, incidents actually seen with my own eyes, that will illustrate the essence of the mood of panic but at the same time will also

---

2 {Before World War II, one of Warsaw's two main Jewish districts was the area around Nalewki Street, now Bohaterów Getta (Heroes of the Ghetto) Street. Yehuda Layb Volman, "Di narshaver nalevkes" ["The Jewish People of Warsaw's Nalewki Street"] in Melekh Ravich, ed., *Dos amolike yidishe varshe: biz der shvel fun dritn khurbn, 1414–1939* [*The Warsaw that Was: Until the Threshold of the Third Catastrophe, 1414–1939*] Montreal: Farband fun varshaver yidn in montreal, 1966), 244–46}, https://www.yiddishbookcenter.org/collections/yiddish-books/spb-nybc205773/ravitch-melech-dos-amolike-yidishe-varshe-biz-der-shvel-fun-dritn-hurbn.

give us the keys to the source of panic among various groups, classes and regions in Poland.

In Peretz's *A Night in the Old Market* produced by the Moscow Granovsky Theatre {in 1925}, there is a scene in the cemetery with zombies wandering around, chasing each other, jumping over each other, catching something in the air, vanishing and suddenly appearing off to the side, from a hole, from a dark corner, seeming to fall down from the heavens, circling each other, whispering and grimacing.[3] Figures in the air, waxen faces, hens' feet, the dead but not dead, the living but not living, bones, skin, dead bodies with living souls, grave dwellers and grave guests, grave aristocrats and grave paupers, early arrivals and latecomers—a commotion, a racket, a din, a fair, a real fair but a cemetery fair, a shadow fair.

One recalls this scene after spending some time in a market in one of the Jewish cities—in Warsaw, Vilna, Bialystok or Lemberg. The picture becomes especially pronounced when one first goes out to such a market on a Sunday, when the long rows of low booths lie as still as tombstones, dead, as if they are hiding something underneath, and afterwards one goes to the same market on a weekday or especially on a fair day and one sees old Jewish women wrapped up in rags; young women with pale, emaciated faces beside a few empty bottles; young women protruding from between strangely coloured pairs of pants and jackets hanging from the booths; boys hopping around with old galoshes in their hands, whispering to you the secret that in a nearby courtyard they can sell you all these goods for a pittance; a hunchbacked old man sitting in a corner repairing shoes; an old woman, half-woman, half-witch, asking you to sample her hot, fresh beans; a mass of persons, perhaps women, perhaps men, throwing themselves at you with requests, proposals, blessings, curses and wild proclamations, the sense of which is difficult to understand. And the deeper one goes, the denser the encampment, the more entangled the skein, the louder the ruckus, the more difficult it is to breathe—a cemetery fair with shadow people and ethereal figures, rag people who move, speak, trade, wander, gesture with their hands and their other limbs. But they do not live.

---

3   Alexis Granovsky and Joseph Gordon, "'Night in the Old Market'. A Mystery in Two Parts after I. L. Peretz," *The Drama Review* (29, 4: 1985), 110.

Not just hundreds but thousands of Jews suckle on this thin cemetery-market's breast. One can estimate that one-eighth of the Jewish population (and no less than one-quarter of Jews considered to be employed in trade) "lives" off these booth-tombstones. And because associations and organizations are now very much in style in Poland, these cemetery people have also organized themselves everywhere in small-merchants' unions.

We will spend only an hour with the reader in the Lvov office of the small-merchants' union. There we will acquaint ourselves with some of this world's living dead. It is Saturday night. The office is packed with Jewish men still in their Sabbath kaftans, threadbare and faded. Their faces are as worn as their kaftans. In a corner, a bunch of women stand separately. They are short, dirty and wrapped in odd shawls so one cannot see their faces. I go into a separate room with the chairman. One by one the applicants are let in. There stands before us a small, thin woman with a large shawl covering her eyes. As she launches into a long, heated speech she starts to move the shawl up and down and we notice that the scrawny, dried up old Jewish woman whom we thought was more than 50 years old is actually still a young woman, between 30 and 35, with young, fresh, lively eyes. She spoke in a way that was a pleasure to hear. But at the same time it made our hair stand on end. She began as follows:

> Jews, you are merciful sons of the merciful! Will you then allow a poor widow to fall into the netherworld? Jews, a poor person like me is as good as dead, but I am not yet dead, and my four children also do not want to die. They eat and peck, but when there is no bread, they eat me, and I will surely soon be dead. Jews, put yourself in my situation, my children have no father and no breadwinner, so be merciful like a father to his sons. Be their father!

I quote almost word for word the language of this young women because I wrote it down that evening. She really poured out everything using Hebrew words and entire biblical quotations, and not just any words and quotations grabbed out of the air, as it were, but always words and quotations that found their mark, truly appropriate to the essence of the matter. When the chairman stopped her and asked her to lay out her request it emerged that she needed to pay the municipal tax collector six *zloty*, and if she didn't pay this "large" sum of money by Monday her "store" would be confiscated—her store consisting of a market stall, which she takes home with her daily, and which is probably worth a total of 10–15 *zloty* from which she and her children "live."

What sort of tax is this? The woman is obliged to pay an annual municipal tax of 60 *zloty* for the right to be a storekeeper in her market stall. She did not pay the tax at the beginning of the year, so the city threatened both to confiscate her "store" and prevent her from working as a storekeeper until she managed to obtain a waiver through a Jewish councilman to obtain the major concession that she would pay the debt of 60 *zloty* over ten months. She had already paid six *zloty* a month for several months on her own. But the last month was especially difficult, so she did not manage to save that sum.

Her husband has been dead for four years. He left her with four tiny children and a promise that in 120 years they would sit together in paradise. Even when he was alive, she was the main breadwinner because the husband studied Torah and earned only a little from tutoring. He was religious and is certainly in paradise, but the misfortune is that his wife, poor soul, is sinful and still lives in this world, and the good children also live and want to know nothing about any crises or tax collectors and want at least a piece of dry bread. How are these weak, innocent babies to blame if there is a crisis in the land and their mother does not earn enough to feed them?

The woman gave a very simple answer to my question of what a crisis is, much clearer than science offers. A crisis exists, she said, when everyone is buried. If I alone were a pauper, things would be bad for me, but it wouldn't be so terrible. I could receive a few *zloty* from someone and borrow some goods to sell. But in a crisis, things are so terrible one might as well stretch out and expire.

The second person to enter the room was a young man, tall and slim, with a white collar and clean, polished shoes—in short, a dandy. He had once owned a shoe business in the middle of the city and was well-to-do. Five years earlier, during the 1925 crisis, he had to close the business and lease a stall where he continued to sell shoes. Last year he had to give up the store and descend another step. He now carries a few pairs of shoes from his home to his booth in the market in the morning and brings them home at night. His foppish appearance is a refugee from his once golden years. Now he is rolling downhill. He has lost all hope of improving himself and has reached a point where he is no longer embarrassed about his condition. For years he hid his misfortune from others and held out hope, but he became more and more indebted until he finally said, "enough passing myself off as someone else, enough pinching my cheeks to bring colour to them and trying to fool others! I must admit to poverty and register in the society of paupers, exposed to the whole world without shame!"

And now a year has passed standing at his booth together with all the *agunes*,[4] widows, invalids, old people, worn out tradesmen, ne'er-do-wells, layabouts, and people who were well-to-do owners before the war but are now over the hill—with all the dregs that the dressed up and painted Jewish centre of Lvov spits out and throws into the garbage heap that is called the market. Every person who goes bankrupt and had no sense earlier to make provisions for himself with a little capital, every person who has been pushed out of the ranks, every person who has fallen down never to stand up again, every hopeless pauper, every Jewess no matter how weak and foolish, every useless idiot—all these people who have been spit out from the centre are thrown together on the garbage heap known as the market and elicit envy from antisemites who complain that the Jews have grabbed the entire market, this garbage-can paradise. And every year we see the addition of hundreds of booths, tables, tents and people who do not even have enough to pay the city for a tiny place of business and are "shopkeepers" with a few old clothes or boots that they carry around and try to sell to "make a living."

Lately, even more people have arrived looking for a place in the garbage can. Some Jews had to flee the countryside because Jews were beaten or because the cooperative tore the last bit of bread from their mouths. So, they set themselves up in the Lvov market. A man does not do so himself because it does not befit him, so he places his wife or his daughter in a booth or a table to "earn a living" until he shows what he is capable of. However, in the end he squanders the goods that he brought from the countryside and becomes a denizen of the market himself.

---

4 {This word has no English equivalent. An *agune* is a married Jewish woman who cannot remarry because she is unable to obtain a rabbinic divorce. Traditionally, divorce must be granted by the husband. In the case of the *agune*, the husband refuses out of spite or has gone missing but his death is unverified.}

And here is the man who has long had tuberculosis, whose irritated eyes scream that he spits up blood. He has been standing for a week by his booth in the cold dampness selling shoes for a total of 46 *zloty*! How much did he profit? Maybe 10 or 15 *zloty*. And he has a wife and two children at home and he himself must drink two glasses of milk every day, for without that he would have been dead long ago.

And what happens later? How does one escape from this grave in which one is buried alive? How does one tear oneself away from the garbage can where the city discards its refuse?

The young man with tubercular eyes spoke as if in a fever. We sat silently as if turned to stone. We let him pour out his heavy heart. We could not interrupt even though we felt that his heated outpouring would cost him more than one glass of blood. He spoke for about a quarter of an hour. He suddenly sat down on a stool and fell silent. Soon he quietly stood up and left the room—asking nothing. The chairman said the following to me:

> With these ones it's worse than with others. They cannot calm down. They feel buried in the market. They keep on shouting from the grave but it doesn't help. It's a grave from which one cannot escape. It is better to lie quietly and not toss and turn.

An elderly Jew in his 60s enters, quietly and embarrassed. He is a shoemaker and he was always a shoemaker. When he was nine years old his father apprenticed him to a shoemaker and since then he has not stopped sewing and patching shoes, formerly for rich people but lately for the poor. But he doesn't complain. He thanks the Lord of the Universe, he is not sinful, but he is old, without the strength to work any longer. He wants to set himself up in the market with some old boots, shoes, and galoshes. He is deaf and believes we are also deaf, so he shouts. He hopes that we can help him rest a little in his old age; he has worked as a shoemaker for 55 years. If he can borrow 25 *zloty* he can establish a used shoe "business" in the market. He is a leather expert and an even bigger expert in boots. He hopes to repay—he will certainly repay—the loan. Why would he not earn enough from a business that allows many Jews to make a living? If there is enough for so many, there will surely be enough for one old Jew who was a shoemaker for 55 years and now wants to rest a little in his final years.

I sat for a few hours in the union office. One after another, Jewish men and women enter. One asks for a few *zloty* to pay taxes. A second requests money for a license, without which his stall will be shut down. A third asks to save him from the tax collector, who has already confiscated his wares. A fourth does not have enough money to buy potatoes early each day from the peasants—he sells them from a wagon that he drives around the city. A fifth, a widow, wants to receive a loan to become a "merchant" in the market. A sixth, the wife of a teacher in a Jewish religious school, wants her daughter, who is already more than 30 years old but cannot get married because she has no dowry, to set up a booth in the market so she can save money for her dowry. And so on.

This social, physical, spiritual and moral refuse comprises up to one-eighth of the Jewish population of Poland's large cities. These widows, orphans, old people, unemployed tradesmen and workers, invalids, physical, psychological and moral cripples, old maids, half-idiotic boys, people who lost their homes during the war, escapees from village life, victims of physical or economic antisemitism—this entire social rabble flows from the city centre to the sewer that is the market.

8. Three-quarters of the Jewish population lack enough to live on

Before the war, the number of rich and middle-class Jews experienced healthy growth. In recent years, too, hundreds of Jews have become rich, built factories and houses, and climbed to a high step on the social ladder. However, these cases are now much less frequent than before the war. Downward mobility is more frequent. The number of rich and middle-class Jews has declined. Wealthy men now fall to the ground precipitously—they fall, sink, and enter the ranks of the poor.

While in Poland I travelled to Otvotsk for a few days to write a couple of articles. Otvotsk is a spa near Warsaw frequented almost exclusively by Jews. The Jewish guesthouses, which are by no means inexpensive, are always full, summer and winter, so it was interesting for me to take a little census at the table where I sat.

Near me sat a Jew, about 45 years old. At first he did not know who I was and I did not know who he was. I had come straight from Lodz, and I told him how antisemitic the Jewish factory owners were in the way they handled Jewish workers. It seems I touched a sore point because he shot back as follows: "One cannot work with Jewish workers. They think more about how to become owners than about work. A contract is not a contract. They do not keep their word. One cannot rely on Jewish workers because they rush to a strike as if it were a dance party." As he fulminated, he mentioned that he owned a large steam mill but hired no Jews.

I let him pour out his heavy heart and then began to tell him about a discussion I recently had in a train with a Polish antisemite. The Christian complained that the Jewish merchant does not think about the quality of his merchandise, only about earning more profit. The Jewish merchant does not keep his word. If he can sell at a higher price to customer B merchandise that he has already promised to customer A, he will find a thousand excuses not to keep his word. He does not think about tomorrow or the day after. He profits even if it comes to blows, and in the end come bankruptcies that ruin the entire trade. The rich miller felt that the Jewish worker is a close relative of the Jewish merchant, really his own flesh and blood, with the same strengths and shortcomings. He then turned the conversation to another theme.

Later I learned that this angry rich factory owner had spent 10 or 12 years as a salesclerk in a mill. He belonged to a socialist party and defended workers' interests reasonably well. He had the good qualities of the Jewish worker. He was well versed in business, no less than the owner. He knew all the firms from which the owner purchased and all the customers to which he sold. He believed in the value of strikes and was the owner's bane.

In the end he became an owner himself, a large, rich, growing factory owner with strong hands and broad ambitions, with the entrepreneurial energy of ten men and hatred for workers, especially Jewish workers. His business grew during the war and the flood of paper money. I spent time with this newly rich man on several occasions. He complained about the crisis, but one got the impression he felt satisfied with the last ten years. The moral of all our talks was that one must be a decent human being, and if one is not a simpleton one can make a living.

I give this example because it is certainly typical. In Poland there are hundreds of newly rich Jews who arose in the bad years, when tens of thousands were downwardly mobile and lost their pre-war assets.

Here in the hotel at his own table sits a Jew, about 50 years old, with a perspiring, nearly bald expanse spread proudly over his narrow head as if declaring to the people around him: "For each hair I lost I made thousands of *zloty*." No matter; for such a price it is worth losing the most beautiful hair. I am not ashamed of my baldness.

Who is he? A former salesclerk from Gensha Street, Warsaw's textile centre, who, during the war, furtively traded in packages of textiles. After the war he opened a textile business of his own. During the period of high inflation, he bought many houses in Berlin for pennies and now they are worth millions. He now resides in Berlin three months a year and trades in everything. If a wagonload of eggs is available, he trades in eggs, if pig bristles {for brushes}, then it's also okay. And lending money with interest or for business partnerships is of course good. The textile business in Warsaw is still in business; it is the prayer and study house that renders all his other businesses kosher. This Jew perspires a lot, but it is a completely different type of perspiration than that of the 70-year-old man who must haul a basket of coal up three stories.

Of 20 guests in the hotel I counted six who became rich after the war. One difference between them and the other 14 is that, before the war, when a Jew's net worth exceeded 100,000 rubles, things continued smoothly. In 90% of cases, growth was assured, and he was certain to become very wealthy. It is utterly different now. The status of half of those who became well-to-do after the war soon falls to that of modest owner or poor man. They make a racket for a few years and their heads spin—not just theirs, but also (and even more) the heads of their wives and children. They learn quickly how to live well, having bigger expenses than rich people had before the war. Then, suddenly, they make a reckoning and find that they have exhausted not only their own assets but also their borrowed money, and they have no way out of this predicament. These entangled rich men are the first candidates for suicide.

In a big city like Warsaw it is difficult to ascertain how many Jews become rich and how many become poor. It is difficult to calculate even for a smaller city. Nonetheless, one can offer a rough sketch that approximates reality.

Consider Pinsk, where there are now around 20 rich Jewish wood merchants. Today, "rich" means having 100,000 or more *zloty* in assets, that is, from $10,000 to $15,000. A couple of wood merchants have even more, up to $25,000. Who are they? Just four of them became rich in the pre-war years, while 16 became rich after the war. Who are the *nouveau riche*? One is a former carpenter, a second a former furrier, a third a former worker on a ship. Well, the tailor and the ship worker at least understand a little about wood and lumber, but how does a furrier enter the trade in wood? It is really a puzzle. However, during the period when the value of money fell, many tricks were played, the statuses of people were rearranged, and worlds were turned upside down.

In Pinsk before the war there were ten Jews who each had assets of a million rubles (that is, $500,000) or more: two bankers, two factory owners, two ship owners, and four large merchants. Now there is just one millionaire, the owner of the match factory, and he does not live in Pinsk.

Before the war there were up to 50 Jews with assets of 50,000 to 100,000 rubles. This prominent group of wealthy men kept on growing. Precise research would allow us to show that nearly every year before the war two or three people were added to this group. Today, this group has nearly disappeared. The rich men are now those with assets of $10,000 to $15,000, and their number is also not large. Before the war one could count a few hundred Jews in this category.

The number of rich Jews and even those who are simply well-to-do has shrunk. The sums that the wealthy own are much smaller than before the war. And the people changed a great deal. From one-half to three-quarters of them entered the *nouveau riche* category after or during the war. They are former salesclerks or artisans, small players with sharp elbows for pushing ahead and long noses for sniffing out a little business under the table.

In Pinsk I was shown an attractive little two-story brick building, recently constructed. In the first story, textiles were sold, and in the second, ready-to-wear clothing. Who are the owners? They are two former salesclerks who, during the war, did not flee although the owners for whom they worked became paupers. They had good relationships with their Jewish and Christian clientele. They started off small but took advantage of the time when the country was flooded with paper money, not only profiting but also constructing buildings and investing in things that maintain their value. The two partners now have the largest and best textile store in Pinsk, and they bless the war, which turned Pinsk on its head, causing the elite to fall to the ground and those on the bottom to rise to the top. This did not occur to all those at the bottom, but a small number of them managed to work themselves up.

Mendele {Moykher Sforim} describes how in {the fictional} Kabtsanok, a wealthy Jewish man emerged overnight, like a cucumber. Just yesterday there was no sign of it and the next day a green cucumber lies in the garden enjoying the warm sun that gave it life and juice. Today's wealthy Jewish men obtained their wealth just like that, but with great effort. Trading in textiles or lumber or grain during the war was a risky enough business, and commerce in the period of high inflation made people nervous wrecks. Today's new rich men therefore have hardened nerves and character. They can pride themselves on the fact that wealth does not fall from the sky, nor does one become rich by miracles. It is a hard undertaking. One must risk one's life. One rides high a hundred times and falls off the horse a hundred times. One is hurled from heat to cold and back again. It is a business that demands patience, daring, talent, and enormous gusto for taking risks.

If the highest step of Jewish economic life fell and grew thinner and smaller, then the lowest step, the poverty step, became much broader and densely populated because it drew on people in all the middle and top steps.

One can imagine economic life as a pyramid with a wide foundation on which the higher steps get smaller as one ascends. For Jews before the war, the middle steps of the pyramid were typically much wider than for other peoples. It is possible that even the highest step was a little wider for Jews. Now, however, the highest step is much more drastically thinned out among than non-Jews. The middle steps also became much narrower for Jews and non-Jews. However, Jews feel the narrowing more than do non-Jews because the middle classes play a larger role in Jewish life. Concerning the lowest step—the poorest masses—the situation among Jews is much worse than it is for non-Jews. The Jews on the lowest step consist of small shopkeepers, minor agents, poorer artisans, and almost all workers. All these classes have in recent years earned barely enough to support themselves or have gone hungry. Among non-Jews, the foundation is composed of workers, peasants, and a small number of urban artisans. Some members of all three groups managed to become officials. They live much better now than before. A small number of peasants entered the liberal professions or became officials, proficient mechanics, workers, traders, or storekeepers. The millions of peasants who own one or two hectares of agricultural land do not live better than the poor Jewish masses in the cities.

Can one measure the number of people who form the poor masses, the breadth of the poverty-stricken foundation on which all the middle and higher classes rest? We will try to do that using Jewish tax lists for Vilna in 1925 and Lemberg in 1928, which we have in our possession. One must note in this connection that the lists consists only of those who own at least a little store or workshop. The poorest are not included—workers and street people who live off of manual labour or incidental precarious employment.

Those whose gross earnings are less than 10,000 *zloty*, that is, less than $1,100 a year[1] are certainly impoverished. In Vilna they comprise more than 84% of all Jewish taxpayers and in Lemberg around 55%. There is no doubt that Vilna is much poorer than Lemberg. However, the cited difference is also due to the fact that 1925 was a terrible crisis year while 1928 was a relatively good year.

Around 26% of Jewish taxpayers in Lemberg and 40% in Vilna have gross earnings of less than 5,000 *zloty* a year. Even if all these taxpayers underestimate their income by 50%, and their retained earnings amount to 20% of their earnings, this means that each of them has retained earnings of 2,000 *zloty* or $220 a year or $18-$19 a month.[2] And these are not individuals but entire families, often large families because, especially in this class, they still believe in the biblical injunction to "be fruitful and multiply" since this is their only pleasure in life.

Let us now consider the very rich, those who stand at the top of the structure of Jewish economic life. These are people whose gross earnings exceed 100,000 *zloty* per year—in Lemberg, 4%, and in Vilna, 1% of Jewish taxpayers. The 4% of rich Jewish Lemberg taxpayers make 37% of all Jewish earnings in the city, while the 1% of rich Jewish Vilna taxpayers make 12% of all Jewish earnings. This shows what a terrible abyss separates the most impoverished from the rich in impoverished Poland.

On average, the very rich Jews have gross earnings of 240,000 *zloty* a year. Even if we accept that none of the very rich underestimated their gross earnings and had retained earnings equal to just 15% of gross earnings, they retained 34,000 *zloty*, or 17 times more than the poorest taxpayers.[3]

By American standards, $3,000 a year is not a large sum, but for Poland it is a considerable amount. However, that is by no means the highest step in the pyramid. In Lemberg, 1% of Jewish taxpayers

---

1 {In January 1928, $1,100 had the buying power of $17,876 in January 2022. US Bureau of Labor Statistics. 2022. "CPI Inflation Calculator," https://www.bls.gov/data/inflation_calculator.htm.}
2 {About $298 dollars a month in 2022.}
3 {It is unclear whether Leshchinsky is here referring to Vilna, Lemberg, or the two cities combined.}

make 20% of all Jewish earnings. Each of these very large merchants or entrepreneurs has gross earnings of 500,000 *zloty* a year and retains 75,000 *zloty*, or 76 times more than Jews in the lowest class of taxpayers.

In the middle lie several classes, poor people and owners, some better off than others. For example, take the poor people who earn twice as much as the poorest of the poor. They earn up to 4,000 *zloty* a year, or up to $40 a month. In Lemberg they constitute 20% and in Vilna 10% of taxpaying Jews. If we combine them with the poorest of the poor, they make up 75% of all taxpayers in Lemberg and 94% in Vilna. This is the broad foundation of Jewish life, and we estimate that the figures for Lemberg are typical for all of Poland. We estimate that another 5–6% of better-off owners make a living, provide for the education of their children, and, with difficulties, get by. And there are an additional 15% of poorer owners, those who toil bitterly to make a living but have enough to eat and dress themselves. Thus, the table on the next page provides a picture of Jewish economic life in Poland that is perhaps not far from reality.

It is interesting that my calculations based on taxpayers in Lemberg are approximately the same as those provided by the manager of the city tax office in Lodz based on the list of Jewish taxpayers in that city. By his count, the Jewish population in Lodz is composed of the following five classes: the poor who pay no taxes (more than 48% of the total); the poor who pay 5 *zloty* in taxes a year (32.5%); people of middling wealth who pay between 20 and 60 *zloty* a year (more than 13%); the well-off, who pay between 100 and 400 *zloty* a year (5%); and the wealthy who pay between 500 and 5,000 *zloty* a year (more than 1%).[4]

---

4 {Elsewhere Leshchinsky provides the income distribution for Jews in Warsaw in 1925 based on an official source: the poor, earning up to 200 *zloty* a month (72.82% of Warsaw Jews); those just managing to get by, earning 200–400 *zloty* a month (17.25%); the middle class, earning 400–1,700 *zloty* a month (9.18%); people of means, earning 1,700–4,100 *zloty* a month (0.65%); the rich, earning 4,100–8,100 *zloty* a month (0.08%); and the economic elite, earning 8,100 or more *zloty* a month (0.02%). Leshchinsky, *Di ekonomishe lage...* [*The Economic Situation...*] op. cit., 52.}

Table 6 Income groups, Polish Jewry, early 1930s, in percent

Income group	Percentage
Poorest of the poor	55
Middling poor	20
Poor owners	15
Middling owners	5
Well-to-do	4
Rich	1
Total	100

Understandably, neither set of calculations can pretend to be perfectly accurate. However, there can be no doubt that they are close to the truth. And the truth is very sad. One is overcome by a sudden shiver when considering that three-quarters of Poland's Jewish population consists either of poor people, who cannot even afford bread, or at best of those that earn barely enough to get by.

It is a wonder that with such poverty and such a small percentage of comfortable and rich Jews, thousands of Jewish institutions are nevertheless maintained in support of religious, social, cultural, hygienic, and various other needs. It suffices to look at a list of social and educational institutions to understand that millions of dollars (not *zloty*) are contributed to the maintenance of these institutions. Polish Jews support 500 cooperative funds; 520 interest-free loan associations; 280 merchant unions; 500 unions of small traders; 100 workers unions; 320 orphans committees; 37 workers cooperatives; and 900 synagogues, *talmud-torahs*, *yeshivas*, and evening courses. These are only a small part of the institutions maintained by Polish Jews. The religious and charitable institutions are much more numerous than others and require serious sums of money. The 500 Jewish *kehiles* in Poland, concerning which reports exist, have a combined budget of more than 30 million *zloty* per year.

The contributions by class to the budgets of *kehiles* are as follows: The rich contribute 25%, the poor contribute 15%, and the middle classes give 60%. The Jewish middle class in Poland struggles continuously with the general economic crises and with crises that are unique to the

Jews and to the middle class. It nonetheless contributes the greatest part of the budget for both the *kehiles* and all other charitable institutions.

It is interesting that the small merchant is poorer than the artisan. This fact jumps out from the tax lists.

9. The destruction of Jewish economic life in Lodz

"The right to work"—this is the great lament of Jewish workers, employees, intellectuals, and the masses who, with each passing day, are pushed further out of the old Jewish professions while being prevented from entering new, modern lines of work. The Jewish masses are simply suffocating in the new social ghetto into which they are being shoved. They are being strangled in the economic ghetto in which they remain trapped.

As I walked along the main streets of Lodz on the day that I arrived, the following phenomenon caught my attention: At almost every gateway, two or three Jewish men stand with a bundle of rope wrapped around their necks. These are Jewish porters, waiting for somebody to summon them to transport a package of merchandise from a factory to a store or from a large store to a smaller one.

The majority are not porters by trade. The latter have an entirely different appearance and work in the factories loading whole railroad cars with merchandise. They are tall young men with broad shoulders, often giants. These men standing by the gateways, on the other hand, look small, thin, and dejected, and it is immediately apparent that they were not born porters. Most are unemployed weavers who have already devoted their last bit of strength to the manufacturers. They are mainly Jewish hand weavers who are without work even as the large factories hum and clatter such a joyous melody for the manufacturers.

These bundles of rope around their necks make a terrifying impression. One must stop and take a good look into the eyes of those wearing the rope around their necks. Alongside me walks a Jewish weaver, a fortunate Jewish weaver who had gotten into a mechanized factory, but who has nonetheless been unemployed for the last three months. He senses that the ropes are tormenting me, pulling me toward the people wearing them around their necks. He comments, as though to himself, "Yes, they've wrapped a rope around the necks of working Jews and keep on pulling it tighter and tighter. They've just about strangled them."

The most terrifying thing is that this rope around the neck of the Jewish worker is being tightened not only by the government, but also by Jews—large-scale Jewish manufacturers, including devout Jews. These devout Jews take the Almighty as a partner in their "noble" trade. They are devout, God-fearing Jews who ostensibly do not want Jews to work on the Sabbath, although their own devout pockets make no distinction between the revenue generated by Sabbath and weekday work. They are virtuous souls who heard back at Mount Sinai that one must keep the Sabbath and then went deaf for the verses about helping a brother. They are Jews with *peyes* and *tsitses* who are frightened of committing the smallest sin, yet their conscience easily bears the death from hunger of thousands of Jewish hand weavers whom they refused to hire when they introduced power looms in their factories.

Whoever has not seen Baluty,[1] the nest of Jewish hand weavers, has not seen the victims of capitalism. In Lodz there are factories, built according to the very latest technology, where 32 looms are run by one worker, where a long hall of 67 by 22 metres is staffed by just 12 people, who only need to monitor and adjust the machines. In the same city, Jewish weavers are dying of hunger, even when the city has a shortage of workers. They work exactly twice as many hours, they sacrifice twice the blood and sweat, standing and working for 16 hours at a time, yet have no money for bread and are literally dying.

I calculated with a Lodz city councillor that Baluty's population is 3.2 times denser than that of the Christian working-class quarter.[2] The

---

1 {Baluty, a neighbourhood of Lodz, was home to many impoverished, working class Jews, including thousands of weavers who worked in cramped apartment sweatshops.}
2 {Leshchinsky writes "32 times denser" but this seems an impossibly high number. Greater London's most densely populated area (Tower Hamlets, the city's second poorest borough, covering most of the traditional East End) is only about seven times more densely populated than its least densely populated borough (Bromley, in the Metropolitan Green Belt, the most rural part of Greater London) (Greater London Authority, "Land Area and Population Density, Ward and Borough," 2022, https://data.london.gov.uk/dataset/land-area-and-population-density-ward-and-borough.}

director of the city's statistical bureau told me that the mortality rate in this part of the city is higher than in any other neighbourhood. One only needs to visit a few apartments in order to catch the whiff of slow death, of expiration.

I visited approximately ten apartments. The picture is the same everywhere: one room, and in that room one or two handlooms. In the same room there is a small bed with a thin straw mattress and a horribly filthy blanket, a stove for cooking in one corner, and everywhere a horde of pale, skinny children with dirty eyes and crooked legs.

The situation of the Christian workers is undoubtedly sad enough. And yet the Jewish workers envy them. First of all, the Christian works in a large factory, which is usually the very last to close, only shutting down when an economic crisis reaches its peak. The small factory or the handloom mill, on the other hand, is the first to cease operations. The Christian worker at the large factory is insured against unemployment and receives support for 17 weeks. The Jewish worker is employed in a small workshop with fewer than five workers and is therefore uninsured. As a result, he begins to go hungry the day he loses his job.

Another important point: the Christian worker's wife or child is also working. Often, one of them works for a state enterprise, on a railroad, or for a municipal enterprise, on a streetcar, in the sewage system, the water system, and so on. It is very rare for all of them to lose their jobs at the same time. Among Jews, the father bears the burden practically on his own, and if he falls, the entire family is ruined.

Walking the streets of Baluty, one sees at every turn groups of Jewish workers, among them many with beards, the fathers of large families. They stand there worried, preoccupied. They cannot afford a single crumb of bread. It is a fact that the peasants who bring their milk, butter, and potatoes to the market in the Jewish workers' quarter have lately been carting their wares back home to the village.

I step into the apartments. Here is a room with two looms. Lying on a dry, thin straw mattress in which there is no longer any straw, a paralyzed woman shouts. She begs God to send the Angel of Death for her as quickly as possible. Her husband died several months ago. Her two sons, hand weavers, went off into the city to look for work. They stand by a gate somewhere with rope around their necks. But very often, the neighbours tell me, they return without a penny, and the paralyzed woman receives nothing. Her cries can be heard the whole length of

Fig. 6 *A street scene, in the Baluty neighbourhood* (1930s), Lodz, Poland. ©Archives of the YIVO Institute for Jewish Research, New York, http://polishjews.yivoarchives.org/archive/index.php?p=collections/controlcard&id=23676

the hallway and the women in neighbouring apartments complain that their children cannot sleep at night.

Here is a second apartment. There is no door. The hole is covered with a sack. Inside is a young woman with four small children. It is cold and the little ones are bundled up in a tattered, dirty blanket. Her husband is on the street. He does unskilled labour for municipal enterprises. The Lodz city council has a socialist majority, and an unemployed Jew can get hired for public works projects. He works just three days a week and earns 23 *zloty*, or $2.50 per week. They are the rich ones of this hallway.

Here is a third apartment. This is the home of a "manufacturer," who has two handlooms and employs a worker. Nobody is working now. He buys wool himself, works it, and sells to stores. A tall Jewish man comes home from the *besmedresh* {prayer and study house} with his *tales* and *tfilin* in hand, speaks little, and makes it clear through his behaviour that he, the "manufacturer," is not—God forbid—to be lumped together with the "proletariat." The woman of the household stands cooking a large pot of potatoes in the same room as the looms.

We continue on our way. Neighbours come out and accompany us. There is only one topic of conversation: Where can one get power looms, and how can one learn to work them? Admittedly, the factories with power looms are also currently shut down, but their workers still had "lucrative" years when they worked without interruption, whereas even in a good year, the hand weavers are without work for nine months. When they are earning, they make just half as much as the workers in the large factories, and when they are not, they are so utterly abandoned that they may as well lie down in the street and die. A power loom or a position in a factory with power looms—that is the dream, the fantasy of everybody languishing and slowly dying in Baluty.

The Joint and ORT have made headway on behalf of Jewish hand weavers and have certainly played a significant role in the hiring of several hundred of them in factories with power looms. In order for weavers to get the chance to use power looms they must learn the necessary skills in the Joint's and ORT's instructional factories; and Jewish manufacturers must hire Jewish workers, since Christian manufacturers certainly will not. However, one can count on one's fingers the number of Jewish manufacturers who do not exclude Jewish workers. To this day, the majority of Jewish manufacturers do not allow any Jews to cross the thresholds of their factories.

The custom of firing Jews and hiring Christians in their place during the transition from handlooms to power looms became the norm in Lodz years ago. The Hershberg and Birnboym firm owned a large factory in Lodz with exclusively Christian workers. The owners were Reform or assimilated Jews. Hershberg decided to open a special factory for Jewish workers. He established a small factory where Jewish hand weavers learned to operate power looms. Gradually, it became a large factory with 166 power looms, all operated by Jews.

Hershberg believed that Jewish workers produced more than Christians and he spread this opinion everywhere. The factory existed from 1912 until the war. It was a Jewish factory not only in terms of the composition of its workers, but also in terms of its spirit. The workers received special permission from the factory inspector to work on Sundays and Christian holidays and rest on the Sabbath and Jewish holidays. There was a small house of prayer for devout weavers. Even the guard in the sentry box who let the workers in and out was a devout older Jew who would recite psalms when he had nothing else to do.

A little while before the war, a rich, devout young man named Budziner became the general manager. The war began and they reduced the number of workers. The general manager fired Jews and hired Christians. He made the excuse that he was afraid of the Christians! After the war, Budziner remained the sole manager of both factories. He closed the Jewish factory. And to this day Budziner does not employ a single Jew among his 300 workers.

This Budziner is not just any old Jew in Lodz. He is a rich, devout man and a member of the Mizrakhi Orthodox Zionist movement. He is the chairman of the Jewish community council and was a member of the Polish senate. This is someone who plays a large role in Jewish communal life. Is such a thing possible among any other nation? Would they not excommunicate such a person? Among us Jews, however, he receives the finest honours in the synagogue, the community council, and even the senate. True, he has two great virtues. He is as devout as can be and as rich as Korakh.[3] But is that really enough for Jews to select him to head the community council and sit in the senate?

Here is a second example: Reb Yekhiel Meyer Pik. He is a Ger Hasid who travels to see his *rebbe* several times a year. He is a member of the *Agudes Yisroel* movement, which wages war for orthodoxy. He has a factory with 120 looms. The master craftsman is a Jew but among 60 workers, there is just one other Jew.

And here is a third—Mr Glikman. He is an active Zionist and a chairman of several Jewish societies, including those in charge of elder and orphan care, among others. He is a real hotshot, and even a bit of a writer, lecturing Jews in a Lodz newspaper and crying that they ought to help sick and old Jews. But among the 200 workers in his factory, there is not a single Jew.

Jews have gotten so used to antisemitism that the most eminent Jewish antisemites occupy the seat of honour in Jewish society and nobody shows them their true place.

This is not just the case with respect to Jewish textile manufacturers. Manual shoemaking is also in the process of disappearing. More and more mechanized shoe factories keep opening, and the manual shoemakers are left without work. In Warsaw, a couple of thousand

---

3 {A figure in *Bamidbar* (the biblical book of Numbers), traditionally viewed as one of the two richest men in the world.}

Jews made their living as shoemakers, producing goods exclusively for export to the Russian provinces. After the war, this trade went through a terrible crisis because the domestic Polish market did not have sufficient demand for so many shoes. Nonetheless, there would still have been a bit of work, since today's Poland is much larger than former Russian Poland. However, there arose another calamity: mechanized shoemaking.

I know of five Jewish mechanized shoe factories in Warsaw in which 520 workers are employed, not a single one of them Jewish. Jewish shoemakers are dying of hunger; they are ready to do gruelling labour just to earn their bread. Representatives of the Jewish professional union beat a path to the doors of the factories, but the manufacturers will not even speak to them.

A turning point has nonetheless been reached with respect to hiring Jewish workers in large mechanized factories. Currently, up to 800 Jewish power loom weavers work—that is, when there is work—in the large factories of Lodz. In Warsaw, two large garment factories with 400 workers have opened and, thanks to the clever tactics and energy of the administration of the Jewish tailors' union, all 400 are Jews. A few Jewish workers have also pushed their way into a couple of new galoshes factories. Thus far, the results have been minimal, but at least it is a start. A possibility has emerged that Jews might penetrate large-scale industry.

This turning point was reached among both Jewish manufacturers and Christian workers. One manufacturer told me that Jewish workers are now a lot calmer, quieter, and less revolutionary than in the past. Why? Because the Jew has so few job opportunities and factory work is such a struggle to come by that he tries much harder than the Christian to stay in his place and—God forbid—not lose his position. Another manufacturer told me that the Jewish worker is more productive because he needs to earn more. He is more willing than a Christian to work overtime and because of this, the machine is in operation longer. A third manufacturer explained that he hires Jewish workers because he does not want to have a double enemy in his factory. The Christian worker hates him both as a manufacturer and as a Jew, whereas the Jewish worker dislikes him only as a manufacturer.

A change has also taken place among the Christian working masses. Thanks to the initiative of the Bund at every convention, congress, city council, and city hall, the Polish socialist worker has finally shifted his position on this issue a little. In 1924, when a Bundist started to speak at a congress of all professional unions about admitting Jewish workers everywhere on an equal basis with Christians, several workers made antisemitic speeches, arguing that Jews could only be found loafing around Nalewki Street, not working. At the latest congresses, there have been no such speeches. The congresses now pass resolutions demanding equal rights for Jewish workers.

In the factories of Lodz, where Christian workers used to go on strike the moment a Jewish worker appeared, the mood has also changed considerably. The Polish workers have come to understand that Jewish workers also have a right to work. Of course, this is far from a unanimous position among Polish workers. Not long ago, the union of antisemitic Polish workers carried out an anti-Jewish demonstration in Lodz, with placards bearing the words, "Down with the Bund and with Jewish workers, who are stealing Christian workers' jobs!" Nevertheless, this iron wall has now also been breached.

The drive of the Jewish masses to work in general, in large factories in particular, is so strong, so intense, that it was inevitable that they would achieve something. How can this be explained? By the immense impoverishment of the Jewish masses.

The standard of living among Jews has declined sharply, and many claim that Jewish labour is now cheaper than Christian labour. Previously, it was always the opposite—Jewish labour was more expensive. But Jews are in such a desperate position, their selection of livelihoods so limited, that they must go to work under the harshest conditions and for the cheapest prices.

It is characteristic that, despite the terrible economic crisis and the immense unemployment, Jews are flocking to ORT courses and asking to learn a trade. A large percentage of them are children of merchants and intermediaries. Out of 242 students, male and female, studying in various ORT trade courses in Lodz, 127 (more than 50%) are the children of merchants, intermediaries, and salesclerks—and that is now, at the time of the most terrible economic crisis.

Let us calculate the level of unemployment among Jews in the two largest Polish centres, Warsaw and Lodz. I acquired these facts in the central bureaus of Jewish professional unions and confirmed them in conversations with the managers.

In Warsaw's knitwear industry, 1,500 of 2,000 Jewish workers (75%) are unemployed. Among the 7–8,000 Jewish tailors in Warsaw, more than 4,000 (55 to 60%) are unemployed. The same is true of 1,600 out of 2,000 gaiter makers (80%) and 1,600 out of 2,000 shoemakers (80%). Out of 2,500 metalworkers, only one-third work a full week; 600 are completely unemployed and 1,000 work half a week. Among 800 leather workers, 70% are unemployed. Thus, in these trades alone, there are more than 10,000 unemployed Jews in Warsaw. We can therefore calculate that the total number of Jews facing unemployment reaches 14–15,000, and including their families, around 50,000. Jewish workers are uninsured. They have no savings because they earn next to nothing. They cannot get hired for municipal work. What option do they have left? Is it any wonder that suicide rates are rising?

Aside from the workers discussed above, there are several thousand Jewish artisans who work at home for the warehouses. They too are impoverished, and a large number are also without work. We can calculate that these artisans plus their families total 20–25,000 people. Thus, among the working class, there are 70–75,000 people going hungry. If we now recall the large mass of small shopkeepers, market stall keepers, and other market vendors who do not earn enough to make a living, our minds are truly left reeling.

In Lodz, there are up to 6,000 Jewish workers in the textile industry, around 4,000 of whom (65%) are unemployed. Of 7–8,000 tailors, 5,000 are unemployed. In all other trades combined, there are up to 5,000 workers, of whom up to 3,000 are unemployed. Thus, in Lodz, there are approximately 12,000 Jews facing unemployment, or 30–35,000 when we include their families.

In Warsaw and Lodz, there are more than 20,000 Jewish salaried employees, of whom approximately 5,000 are unemployed.

Thinking about the vast army of unemployed Jews is enough to make one's hair stand on end. They are absolutely defenceless and receive no support from the government. They have only one way out: death from hunger or suicide.

Unemployment, as with the economic crisis in general, has certainly also impacted the Christian population, but their situation is not as desperate. Eighty percent of the non-Jewish population makes a living from agriculture. It is undoubtedly a great catastrophe for them that grain prices are so low that they lack money for clothing, farm improvements, and so on. However, they are not going hungry.

Just 2% of non-Jews work in commerce, compared to 36% of Jews. Eight percent are involved in industry and, even then, mostly in large-scale industry, which grants all unemployed workers state support. Among Jews, the percentage in industry is 4.5 times greater, but these Jews work only in skilled crafts and small-scale industry, so they are not entitled to unemployment insurance. Fully 6% of non-Jews are employed by the state as officials and workers, and even during the greatest crisis they receive their pay and live in security. Not even 1% of Jews are employed by the state. In Galicia, there are still a few Jewish officials left over from the old days,[4] but they are gradually being replaced, and the day is not far off when former Galicia will become identical to former Russian Poland, where there was not a single Jewish official.

The role of state officials should not, however, be measured according to their number. Their role is much larger, and the greatest tragedy of Polish Jews is indeed the fact that the state machinery lies in the hands of those who are not only antisemitic, but in general do not have the faintest clue of the complexity of a modern state's workings. All of the state's apparatuses are not only ethnically, but also socio-communally hostile toward Jews. The majority of officials are the children of landowners, the nobility, and newly-rich peasants, all people who are far removed from commerce and industry and hostile toward such livelihoods. They grew up in a milieu that viewed urban occupations with detached antagonism, and in the city, too, they live in an environment disconnected from commerce and industry. People like these are the ones determining the fate of the two fields in which 75% of Polish Jews make their living. It is therefore only natural for the state to wage a constant war against Jews, in whose hands commerce and industry primarily lie. And since Jews are even more involved in commerce than in industry, the greatest fury is directed toward the merchant class, which in Poland is 65–70% Jewish.

The Polish official never comes into any contact whatsoever with merchants, and he therefore has no sense of their good times or their bad. He carries out his duties not as a living person with feelings and sympathies, but as a machine, a cold mechanical apparatus, and for this

---

4 {Until 1918, Galicia was part of the Austro-Hungarian Empire. Galician Jews were officially granted full rights in 1867.}

reason behaves mercilessly and cruelly. In many cities where the Polish population is an insignificant minority and the Jewish population a vast majority, the Polish officials sent there end up feeling like occupiers, like an army that has conquered a foreign land. They give no consideration whatsoever to the interests of the population, focusing solely on the interests of the position entrusted to them.

The struggle among Jews for the right to become state officials is perhaps the most important one in the general struggle for the right to work. The right to work—this is now the urgent cry of the entirety of Polish Jewry. This cry is directed toward the state, the city councils, the manufacturers, and, more than anyone else, the Jewish manufacturers.

It is not only that Jews are not hired as state officials; they are also barred from work as municipal officials, and even from work for municipal enterprises such as streetcars, sewage systems, or water systems. They are not even permitted to clean the streets, although Jews are pleading to do this kind of unskilled labour.

Table 7 Percent Jews and Jewish municipal workers and officials by city

City	Percent Jews	Percent Jews, municipal workers and officials
Warsaw	32.5	3.0
Lublin	34.0	2.6
Ostrovets	33.0	1.1
Aleksandrov	30.0	4.0
Konin	33.0	2.9
Mishtsanov	50.0	1.0
Lipno	25.0	8.0
Khelm	50.0	12.0
Naselsk	55.0	10.0
Navidvar	60.0	11.0
Byala	50.0	15.0
Vladimir-Volynsk	70.0	16.0
Grodne	47.0	10.5
Rovne	75.0	13.0
Hrubeshov	60.0	70.0
Slonim	70.0	51.0

The table immediately above is based on facts assembled by the Bureau for the Right to Work. Only in a couple of cities do Jews comprise a significant percentage of municipal workers and officials. In most cities, Jewish municipal workers and officials are one-tenth to one-fifteenth as numerous as the percentage of the Jewish population overall. The Bundist faction of the Warsaw city council has been fighting resolutely for several years for the hiring of Jewish workers and officials, but so far has had virtually no success. The couple hundred Jews who are counted in Warsaw as municipal workers are employed in the Jewish hospital and orphanage, which are under the authority of the city council.

A kind of alliance has developed between devout Jewish manufacturers and the antisemitic politics of the state and city halls, and it is left to the Jewish masses to fight against it. This fight is a matter of life and death.

10. Fallen Jewish Vilna

Vilna is now a dead city. For a newcomer, the streets immediately make a frightful impression. In truth, the sidewalks are a little fixed up and the houses are somewhat washed and cleaned. However, the *people* in the streets look more dejected, fallen, and neglected than they did three years ago. There is no city in Poland where people are so poorly dressed. People's clothes are so worn that poverty seems universal. Poverty is a resident, a secure owner in the city, and is not of two minds about leaving here. People in Vilna have come to accept this situation. Privation stretches out broadly, dominating every aspect of life. There are no hopes, no prospects, so one must make peace with destitution.

In no other city of Poland does one see as many closed and bolted stores as in Vilna. On Strashun Street I counted 16 such stores out of 42. On the street of the Vilna Gaon,[1] one of every four or five stores is closed—similarly on Daytsher, Zavalner Street, and Troker Street.

True, I was in Vilna at the end of January, in the month when one must renew {business} licenses. It is possible that many storekeepers will eventually receive enough money from America or a credit fund to renew their licenses. But in itself, the fact that one is forced to close up shop for a month or two demonstrates how profoundly destitute the population is. In the merchants' union they gave me to understand that this January 352 stores and 60 workshops were closed because their owners could not afford license renewals. How many will eventually be able to reopen and how many will abandon their boarded-up doors and seek new livelihoods one cannot yet know. The closed stores make an impression similar to the scene immediately following a pogrom, when not everyone has returned to the city and not all inheritors have opened up the stores of their murdered parents.

---

1 {Eliyahu ben Shlomo Zalman, the Vilna Gaon (genius), was a leading eighteenth-century Talmudist and proponent of *misnagdic* (anti-Hasidic) Jewry.}

The Jewish population, which is tormented by the tax collector and ruined by antisemitism, certainly feels as if it has endured a pogrom, a tax pogrom that has gone on for years and for which one sees no end. I first felt the tragedy of the tax- and antisemitism-pogrom when I began to enter stores that were open for business.

Many residents of Vilna certainly remember Zalkind's large store. It existed for more than a century, surviving good times and bad, times of expansion and crisis. But then the business arrived at the period of antisemitism and tax pressure after Poland became independent.

Before the war, up to 150 people worked in Zalkind's business—clerks, bookkeepers, and ordinary workers. It was a large clothing and haberdashery business with its own workshop with 50 tailors. The business occupied a large three-story building and always seemed lively, fresh, growing, and successful.

When I entered the store, I was astonished. Deep in the store it was dim. The top floors were dark. For a distance of several steps after the entrance, the store was illuminated. A man with a bandaged head was wandering around. His eyes jutted out prominently. They peered into the distant darkness and then wondered at the stranger entering the store and disturbing the grave-like stillness. Two other men stood by the checkout. They leaned against the wall—quiet, frozen, as if condemned. Two young women stood by the shelves. They were startled when I entered, not used to being disturbed.

The three men were the owners. The two young women were the last of the many clerks. They were the last flickering candles that will probably be snuffed out because the store must close down. The word "catastrophe" is too weak for the situation I encountered in the store, where to be served one used to have to wait for a long time until one of the clerks was free.

I grew depressed from the darkness, emptiness, stillness, and the quiet steps of the owner with the bandaged head, who moved around like a shadow, a symbol of life extinguished. I spent a long time in the store and had a long discussion with the owners about the factors that ruined such a sound and reliable business. Here they are:

The war was already a resounding blow because the population became impoverished. Vilna was near the front and was often cut off from the world. Afterwards inflation arrived. Merchandise became scarce and paper billions mushroomed. When the value of the currency, the *zloty*, was established {in 1924}, one received little merchandise of little worth. These were certainly big blows that weakened the business's capital. But all these setbacks did not ruin the business. It was laid waste by factors of an entirely different character.

Zalkind's business depended mainly on consumers comprised largely of Russian officers and officials from tens of state institutions. They made purchases without money, on instalment, and bought in the same store for decades. All of these customers are now gone. Polish officers and officials buy from Jews only when they lack an alternative. However, such cases are fewer every day. Polish-owned stores are opening, taking the place of the Jewish-owned stores.

In no city is the competition from new Polish storeowners felt more keenly than in Vilna. A good Polish haberdashery was established just in the last few years, and it diverted revenue that formerly went to Zalkind. A new Polish textile store was also established. It siphoned off the best Polish customers of dry goods. A new Polish business specializing in pharmaceuticals was also established, and the respected pharmaceutical business of the Jewish Segal brothers is wavering and shrinking from day to day. The Segal brothers are well-known Zionists. One of them now lives in the land of Israel, where he has many gardens and where his son tragically died in the last pogrom in Palestine. Before the war, Segal's business in Vilna had up to 100 employees. Now it has fewer than ten.

The Polish storekeeper is often victorious against his Jewish counterpart because the Polish state is on his side. Here is an example: The Railway Directorate sent its officials a circular in which it recommended that they buy from Polish storekeepers. The circular does not say they should boycott Jewish storekeepers, but the Polish official easily surmises what is meant and is gladly ready to carry out the good deed of pushing Jews out.

Similarly, Bank Polski, the state bank, is in pure Polish hands, so a Polish storekeeper receives more credit more frequently and easily than does his Jewish counterpart. The kind of credit policy followed by the Polish state bank becomes clear from the fact that in 1929 it issued credit totalling 103 million *zloty* in Lodz and 312 million *zloty* in Posen. One does not need to study Polish economic life thoroughly to know that

Posen does not have even one-quarter of the industry of Lodz. Lodz is second only to Warsaw in the amount of tax on gross sales that it contributes to state coffers; Posen is in fifth place. Why then does Posen receive three time more credit than Lodz does? Perhaps Lodz is so rich that it does not need so much credit? It emerges that even the world-famous Poznanski textile factory {in Lodz} discounted promissory notes on the stock exchange at more than 20%. Once can therefore imagine what kind of need exists in Lodz for credit. One must therefore look for another explanation, and it is not hard to find. In Lodz all factory owners with very few exceptions are Jews and Germans, not Poles. And in Posen there are few Jews—even few Germans remain there.

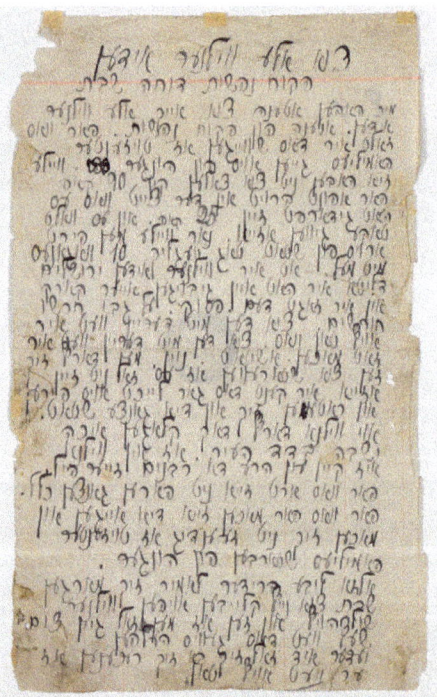

Fig. 7 Untitled handwritten appeal (1923?), Vilna, Poland. ©Archives of the YIVO Institute for Jewish Research, New York. The appeal states: "To all Vilna Jews: saving souls is more important than keeping the Sabbath. We have a grievance against all Vilna Jews. The grievance concerns saving souls. Why should you be silent when thousands of Jewish families are starving?" The appeal singles out rabbis for ignoring the plight of families dying of hunger and calls on Jews to gather in a synagogue courtyard the next day, on the Sabbath, to address the issue. The appeal refers to a 360% increase in the price of a funt (0.41 kg) of bread, suggesting that it may have been written during the hyperinflation of 1923, http://polishjews.yivoarchives.org/archive/index.php?p=collections/controlcard&id=21092

Let us return to Vilna. One can see an example of how the Jewish artisan suffers from antisemitism from the following fact: Before the war, there were 300–350 Jewish painters in Vilna. They worked mainly on the railway line, state secondary schools, and also private buildings. The state was the largest construction enterprise. Today, Jews are not hired to do state work. Even city hall seldom gives Jews a little work. Accordingly, there are now in Vilna just 40 Jewish painters and 30 apprentices. Before the war, Christian painters were just one-fifth or one-sixth as numerous as Jewish painters. Today, there are ten times more Christian than Jewish painters. Before the war there was one Jewish contractor who had 80 Jewish workers. Now there are almost no Jewish entrepreneurs in this field. All Jewish painters are individuals who work with one apprentice.

Almost the same thing happened with carpenters. Before the war, there were 300–350 Jews in this trade. There were three big factories that employed more than 200 workers. Now there remain only 50–60 Jewish workers distributed over many small workshops. Meanwhile, the number of Christian carpenters has increased considerably. The only explanation is that private individuals build little and seldom. Only the state and the city build much, and they do not employ Jews.

The province of Vilna was always rich with forests. As everywhere in Poland, the lumber trade lies completely in Jewish hands. In the city of Vilna alone there are even now about 200 large and small lumber merchants with about 400 employees. All without exception are Jews. In the entire Vilna area about 1,000 Jews, owners and employees, earn a living from the lumber trade. Including their families, they number about 4,000 people because they are mainly Jews with large families. Around these 4,000 Jews are another 1,000 or so Jews working as dealers and artisans.

Recently an edict was issued to stop selling state-owned forests. The Jews greeted it like a thunderbolt but for Christian forest workers the situation is now better. The state will surely pay no worse than Jewish private entrepreneurs. However, laws concerning the length of the workday and insurance will be better respected. In place of 500–600 Jewish employees there will probably be no fewer than 1,000 Christians. Therefore it is not just the Jewish bourgeoisie that pays the price of nationalization but also Jewish workers.

To form a picture of the tax collectors as real murderers, it is enough to hear out just a few Vilna Jews about the taxes that are torn from the population. They are actually the main force driving Jews to suicide. It has progressed to the point that in Vilna a Christian storekeeper by the name of Dukovski committed suicide and left a letter to the Finance Department saying that he is departing the world because he can no longer afford to pay taxes. This one and only Christian suicide (compared to the tens of Jewish suicides) caused such an uproar that the entire Polish press reported it. As long as only Jewish merchants and storekeepers were throwing themselves from the upper stories and splitting open their heads, all Polish newspapers kept quiet.

One must understand that, in general, tax fees are much lighter for the Christian than the Jewish merchants and storekeepers. When I was in Poland, barely a day passed where in one place or another a Jew did not commit suicide because of taxes. In Lemberg, a mother of six children hanged herself after tax collectors removed the last bit of merchandise from her store. Interestingly, even a Polish National-Democrat, who according to his program must be an antisemite, broke down in tears at Warsaw City Hall when a Bundist read a document outlining how they took the last sack of potatoes from a Jewish family in lieu of taxes.

A Lodz merchant who travelled with me from Lodz to Warsaw told me the following characteristic story: He owns a textile store in Lodz. In the last two years he paid 1% of his gross income in tax because he is a wholesaler. Soon a new tax inspector came and decided that he is not a wholesaler but a retailer and must therefore pay 2.5% of his gross income. He was ready to pay the amount due when the inspector declared that he must also pay additional percentage points and fines for the last two years, amounting to exactly twice as much as the previous total.[2] The merchant was hurrying off to Warsaw to ask the minister not to ruin him and turn him into a poor man. But there was faint hope that he would be heard and that it would be decided that the problem was the tax inspector, not the merchant. Such cases number in the hundreds and thousands. It is enough to say that in the last few years tax officials collected 200 million *zloty* more than was designated—all blood drawn from Jewish storekeepers, often small ones.

---

2 {These percentages seem small but it is unclear how often they were collected and how small the merchant's margins were.}

When the previously mentioned Christian storekeeper in Vilna committed suicide, nearly all stores in the city were closed for the funeral, which was attended by a huge crowd. In this manner they at least protested against the inhuman actions of the tax officials. But when a Jew jumps from the fifth story because the tax officials took everything from him, he is buried quietly somewhere behind a fence. His relatives are too ashamed to say that their father or uncle departed the world because of tax murderers. A few years ago, the rabbis even issued an appeal not to {religiously} honour a person who commits suicide because suicides have no life in the hereafter.

If one wants to see how Vilna is going under it is enough to sit for half an hour in the office of the *gmiles khsodim* {benevolent society} fund or the emigration office. Lending 50 or 100 *zloty* without interest to be repaid in small sums is the aim of the *gmiles khsodim*, which the "Joint" supports in hundreds of Jewish towns and which is now the most popular and loved institution everywhere (see fn. 1, p. 60). The fund was created for the weakest and poorest parts of the Jewish population in Poland. Among the latter, five or ten dollars is a significant amount of "capital" that cannot be obtained elsewhere. Their entire existence depends on such amounts.

The *gmiles khsodim* fund in Vilna does a very good job of rescuing the small storekeepers that have 50 *zloty* worth of merchandise, the women who sell fruit or chickens, the cobblers, and ordinary poor artisans. However, while it is designated for the poorest people, those who in normal times would be embarrassed to visit its office also seek assistance from the fund. I sat there and saw one man requesting a loan of 100 *zloty* ($11) because he could not afford to renew his business license and without the renewal he would have had to close his store. Artisans arrive who just a couple years ago employed two or three workers and enjoyed a good income. Teachers, salaried employees, workers, and, in truth, members of all classes enter. And if until last year everyone paid up when a loan repayment was due—because they knew for certain that they would get the hundred or fifty *zloty* again as soon as they settled up—now the situation is much worse. There are twice as many overdue and unredeemed promissory notes as those that are paid off by the due date.

In the waiting room of the emigration office I met a large crowd. Almost all the people were youthful, between 25 and 30 years old, men and women. I asked a young man of about 25 if he has anyone in Brazil, where he wanted to go. His answer was curt: "I am traveling to God. I have nobody there, but here I have nothing." This was the mood of everyone in the waiting room—they were eager to move to the ends of the earth just to stop fading out and going under in Vilna, where people had given up hope and ceased to believe in better times. Vilna's Jews migrate to remote parts of the world, to South America, Central America, Africa, and Australia to anywhere ships and trains go. Vilna's Jews have beat a path to places where Jews have never been.

The Jews of Vilna do not lack energy and courage. Here before me stands a young woman, who looks about 19 years old although actually she will be 21 in a few months. Her father is in New York and he wants to bring her over. The American consul requires clear proof that she is not older than 21 but she has only a certificate from her *shtetl*'s rabbi. And in two months she will lose her right to go to her father in New York. A more desperate face is difficult to imagine. The young woman was really trembling and barely holding in her tears. And she was not the only such case.

I was told also in Warsaw, Lemberg, and Bialystok that the American consul torments the unlucky prospective emigrants who by law have the right to be admitted first into the quota. Among all these young people who lack official documents testifying that they are younger than 21, the consul intentionally introduces difficulties so that the term permitting entry into the United States will expire. In the Warsaw office I saw a young man who was two weeks away from losing his right of entry. In the space of two weeks it was impossible for him to prepare as many documents as the consul demanded. The young man argued, begged, and made plans but the manager of the office had to explain plainly that his running to lawyers would be a waste of money and effort. One felt that this was the end of the young man's one and only hope, the loss of his years-long dream and therefore of everything, of the one opportunity to make something of his life. It had been five years since he completed his schooling, and during that period he had waited and looked forward to the moment when his turn would come and he would escape to his father in New York. I am sure that the young man did not receive a visa. I am not sure that he is still alive. His face was too desperate, his spirit too dejected.

In Vilna, all classes are dejected and impoverished. Understandably, there are still some rich people. However, they are so insignificantly small in number that one does not feel their presence in the city. And they, too, are sinking. In all cities there are plenty of Jews who have gone downhill but in Vilna there remains no sign of once rich people. In Warsaw, Lodz, Krakow, Lemberg—everywhere in cafes and restaurants I saw many Jews, many richly dressed Jewish women. But in Vilna one finds no Jews in the better restaurants. I purposely went to the few restaurants where at night there is music and dancing. I found no Jews there. In general, one sees only officials and officers in restaurants. In contrast, even in this difficult time, the most expensive cafes and restaurants in Warsaw are packed, mostly with Jews.

Why has Vilna suffered more than other cities? Warsaw, Lodz, Radom, Bialystok, and other cities lost a lot when the Russian market for their merchandise was no longer available. However, while the other cities gained markets in Posen, Upper Silesia, and Galicia, compensating to a great extent for the loss of the Russian market, Vilna lost everything.[3] It is situated far from the new Polish markets and so cannot compete with other cities that are situated closer to them. Apart from chamois and glove makers, who sell large amounts of merchandise in Posen, no other article that used to be made in Vilna found a place in the new Polish markets. The sock industry, which used to employ thousands of people, is completely dead. Ready-to-wear clothing production is nearly dead. Tanneries are on their death bed. And so it is in all branches of trade and industry. Vilna lost not only the Russian market, where it used to send ready-to-wear clothing, shoes, socks, and leather, but also nearby markets. The Kovno, Minsk, and Vitebsk governorates used to be major consumers of Vilna's products. Now they are torn away and cut off from Vilna.

Walled off by borders from all areas with which Vilna traded for centuries, and in particular from the Russian market, for which Vilna was producing more and more in the decades before the war, Vilna

---

3 {The new markets became available after World War I, when Poland gained new territories along with independence. The Russian market was lost during Poland's 1919–21 war with Russia.}

is also now far from the rich Polish market. It is wedged in a narrow corner, exhausted by the war, suffocating from antisemitism, drained by taxes. Once rich Jewish Vilna lies sick and weak, beaten and fallen, without hope for better and brighter times.

11. The superfluous

I do not know whether fish in the sea tremble the whole month of *elul*.[1] However, I have no doubt that most Polish Jews tremble even now, genuinely fearing God and believing that one is whipped in the hereafter for sins and sits in paradise for good deeds. No part of the Jewish people has demonstrated such stubbornness, obstinacy, spitefulness, and conservatism as Polish Jewry.

Overnight, before my eyes, young men in tens of Ukrainian hamlets cut off their *peyes*, shortened their caftans, threw their *tefillin* in the attic, sent their daily and high-holiday prayer books away with the itinerant bookseller, shouted at their grandparents not to interfere in their affairs—and became "gentiles." They knew Russian, devoured the Russian writers Pushkin and Lermontov, wore Russian shirts, ate pork enthusiastically, and on Rosh Hashanah and Yom Kippur went for walks in the forest around town, grazing on little livers and gizzards that they brought with them from the *kapore*[2] at home. Their fathers and mothers often did not even protest. They groaned and sighed, bemoaning the fact that they did not have enough sense to act accordingly in their young years.

Here, in Poland, they have been cutting off *peyes* for more than a century, tearing strips off long coats, bombarding prayer and study houses with *haskala*, enlightenment, assimilation, socialism, and communism, attacking Hasidic rabbis with large philosophical books and small trashy brochures about the mysteries of the Turkish court. They have been flooding the *yeshivas* with serious and poisonous literature,

---

1 {Rosh Hashanah and Yom Kippur, the "Days of Awe," take place in the month of *elul* in the Jewish lunar calendar. According to a Yiddish saying, "Even the fish in the sea tremble as the Days of Awe approach."}

2 {A traditional atonement ceremony in preparation for Yom Kippur involved the ritual slaughter of a chicken, the *kapore*.}

and setting evil forces on the *yeshiva* students. Yet, every time I come to Warsaw, Lodz, Lemberg, Kiev or Krakow, to Kutne or to Vlotzlavek, I find that the long coat still dominates the picture. The orthodox, religious Jews control the communities. The Hasidic rabbis rule over minds and souls and are followed fervently by thousands and tens of thousands of people, who follow to the point of risking their lives. I still meet eight- and nine-year-old boys with *peyes* all the way down to their necks and young wives with wigs drooping over their eyes. I still see packed little houses of prayer and study. And the dancing and fervent singing in small Hasidic houses of prayer during the Sabbath evening meal resound and overpower the songs and shouts of all national and socialist groups and circles.

Of course, struggling will not help. The Angel of Death of assimilation does its work diligently and thoroughly, especially the Angel of Death of linguistic assimilation. The picture is changing, and the worm eats its way into the body of Polish Jewry. But for the time being, religious Jews are the majority. Polish Jews are the only Jewish community in the world that has a religious youth, a youth that is consciously faithful to the old, deep-rooted customs and defends and promotes them both with the most modern measures and measures employed by their grandparents.

Here, among these devout, God-fearing Polish Jews, and precisely in the month of *elul*, there were so many and such frightful suicides that one cannot keep silent. One cannot and one must not keep silent, even when one knows one can be of no help. One must not tire of shouting that, apart from poverty, hunger, and need, which can certainly lead to suicide, Polish Jews are spiritually sick from despair, hopelessness, lack of prospects, helplessness, disorientation, and lawlessness. In tens of cases one could with a small sum or a brotherly hand save someone from death, perhaps return the appetite and the desire for life.

"I decline such a life! Let me die!"—thus shouted a Jewish girl who had drunk a bottle of carbolic acid and whom a doctor was trying to save. "I decline such a life! Let me die!"—screams out from each Jewish suicide. It seems that people simply no longer have the physical and spiritual strength to struggle for a dry crust of bread and a roof over their head. They can no longer endure the grief of their hungry, blameless children. Dying is the best solution, the only way out.

Here is a characteristic tragedy from Warsaw that cost the life of a very young person, a person who had not yet tasted life's riches. Yosef Vasershteyn and his wife, Pesl, lived at 48 Shliske Street. They were married a mere 20 months earlier and Pesl was just 21 years old. Both of them were merchants in the market.

God sent Vasershteyn a big deal—Vasershteyn bought tomatoes at a low price and hoped to profit enough to buy food for the Sabbath and Rosh Hashanah, which came right after. But a person plans and the police laugh. Just as Vasershteyn appeared on the street with a basket, he fell into the hands of a police officer, who hauled him off to jail. Street trade is forbidden, and thousands of Jews therefore run around illegally with their baskets—running, hiding, falling into the hands of the police, bribing their way out, and hurrying off again with their baskets over the streets and the courtyards, plying their trade and bringing something home in the evening. May Hitler have no more and may Goebbels be no more satisfied—but one lives! However, Vasershteyn met a wicked police officer and remained imprisoned for two days, Friday and Saturday.

This was not such a misfortune! The young wife immediately knew where she could find her husband and was herself ready to be sentenced. A person does not suffer much from sitting a few days under lock and key. However, tomatoes are more delicate than people are and cannot endure the suffocating and smelly air of a Warsaw jail; tomatoes tend to rot. And Sunday, when Vasershteyn was freed, he brought home rotten tomatoes. That was their entire capital, the only hope of providing for the holiday! They had secured the capital by pawning his wife's one and only coat.

The wife's nerves could not stand it. She tore the clothes she was wearing and tried to jump from the third floor. Her husband stopped her and calmed her. Neighbours brought five *zloty*, providing capital so they could continue their business, but the fate of the wife was already determined: for the five *zloty* she did not buy delicate tomatoes, which rot quickly, but a large quantity of carbolic acid. She drank it so quickly and completely that no medication and no shouts could awaken her. The neighbours say her husband was jealous of her, {believing that} she had overcome all and was rescued.

At 45 Genshe Street in Warsaw lived 43-year-old Yitskhok Berlinerbloy, a merchant. He was married and had a 10-year-old son. He dealt in linen and was known as an honest, decent, and calm man. Four days before Rosh Hashanah, Berlinerbloy left his house, walked two houses down the street, went up to the third floor, and threw himself down so successfully that his whole head scattered into pieces and he died immediately. The cause? Need, fear of the next day, spiritual disorientation, hopelessness.

That same day at 6 Kempne Street, 50-year-old street trader Mendl Gutshtat threw himself from the fourth story. He died in hospital. And at 19 Muranov Street in Warsaw, 20-year-old Yekhiel Skorokhud jumped from the fourth floor. He was an upholsterer. For years he went hungry, but quietly and without complaint. Only at the time of his death did he hit the stones of the courtyard with a thud strong enough to awaken his neighbours at 4 a.m., declaring: "Forgive me for such a life! I decline such a life!" A day later, Ben Tsien Mushinski jumped into the Vistula and drowned. He was an intellectual who sold magazines and subscriptions {for a living}. Lately he had quietly been starving. His acquaintances believe he had long been for the next world, had long regarded himself as superfluous.

The superfluous number not in the thousands nor in the tens of thousands but perhaps in the hundreds of thousands. That is maybe the greatest curse, the most terrifying obscenity—to be superfluous. There are many types, degrees, and stages of superfluity. Some feel superfluous only in Poland, and believe that in another place they can still live and be useful. However, others believe that they are completely superfluous in the world. The most courageous of the superfluous draw the logical conclusion. The weak and the broken drag themselves around but ask themselves what they can accomplish, what they can achieve as a result of their struggle.

Lodz competes with Warsaw. Precisely a week before Rosh Hashanah the 52-year-old butcher Kukhtshik hanged himself in his butcher shop— on a hook on which he used to hang meat. He was once a proprietor but business was poor. He left a wife and several children. He did not utter a word at home, left for his butcher shop early, locked himself from the inside and bid farewell to the world. The family members felt a disquiet, a fear, a call to the butcher shop. They all ran there and met their dead husband and father hanging on the hook where for 30 years he had hung slaughtered oxen. And in truth, how is a man more important than an ox? Especially a superfluous man?

That same day in Lodz, 23-year-old Hersh Margolis, the son of respectable parents, hanged himself over 50 *zloty*. He left a little note saying that nobody is to blame for his death. Nobody? Yes, the superfluous blame no one, they depart and clean up their path. They leave without anger and without protest—if one does not count their departure itself as a protest.

12. Emigration tragedies

Recently, I happened to read an article in a Yiddish newspaper about emigration. The author said so easily, so casually that actually there is no emigration at all now; where is there for Jews to go? What is the point of all the committees that are supposedly taking care of Jewish emigrants and helping to create opportunities for immigration?

I read the article right after I had returned from a trip to Poland to visit the Jewish emigration offices. I thought about how good it would be if a large number of American Jews could be brought there, at least for a couple of hours, to sit and look into the eyes of the men, women, and adolescent girls and boys. They would read in their eyes such desperation, sorrow, and worry, such a longing for rest and a sure source of bread. They would immediately understand how massive and how urgent the emigration question is for the millions of Jews from Poland, Romania, Lithuania, Latvia, and certainly Russia as well, if only it were possible to leave.

It would be sufficient for the American Jews to sit there for a little while and look into the eyes of these many living souls being extinguished by destitution and adversity, yet fiercely longing to tear themselves from their predicament, to leap out of the chasm of poverty and reawaken their creative forces and energy. I would sit them down at the reception desk and let them look through a few of their document packages.

Every one of them would recognize that the 40,000 Jews currently emigrating each year generate a thousand times more work, more suffering, more hardship, more hustling, more tears, more hassles and headaches, than a million Jewish emigrants did before the war. Every emigrant creates a mountain of hardships, from extricating a simple document from a police clerk to pushing through the narrow gates of the destination country.

Before the World War, all the hardships related to crossing the border; the tsarist regime also forbade emigration from Russia. Once people crossed the border, they were as free as birds and could travel wherever they desired. Visas were not necessary. Now, however, the consulates of the destination countries have become sites where poor emigrants are harassed. They are genuine Inquisition institutions where they put emigrants through the wringer and subject them to hellish torment.

Let us consider a few real-life examples. Here is a fifteen-year-old girl. Her name is Rivke Blumvald and she comes from Shedlets. Her parents escaped to Russia when the Germans occupied Shedlets in 1915, leaving their several-month-old daughter with relatives. After the war ended, the relatives also departed for Russia, but since they knew nothing about the child's parents, they left her behind in Shedlets. A family took her in out of pity for the "orphan" whose parents were still alive.

After much correspondence and searching, HIAS managed to find the child's parents in America, where they had immigrated after the war.[1] A stroke of luck! A cause for celebration! But the consul does not want to permit the "orphan" to finally see her parents and embrace her own mother after 15 years of wandering among strangers.

There arises the problem of documentation proving that this Rivke Blumvald really is the daughter of the Blumvalds in the United States. The whole story with escaping to Russia, leaving behind a child, living with strangers for 15 years, miraculously finding the parents all of a sudden—this all sounds to the consul too much like a legend for him to believe it straightaway. Rabbis must testify under oath and mountains of papers must be provided from various police departments and courts. Finally, God softens the consul's heart and he agrees to give her a visa.

There is cause for celebration after all! All the employees of the emigration bureau are ready to dance for joy along with the girl. They know very well the suffering and anguish of this child, who has never known the feeling of having a father and mother. But a person plans and God laughs. At the last minute, there is a new ordeal—her eyes are not entirely healthy and must be treated for several months. More

---

1 {HIAS is an abbreviation for the Hebrew Immigrant Aid Society, a Jewish-American organization founded in 1881 to provide aid to Jewish immigrants to the United States.}

hardship, more tears. But the committee is keeping her hope alive, and I am certain that she will eventually enter Columbus's Garden of Eden. Rivke Blumvald will make it to her parents in America.

In recent years, a couple of thousand Jews have immigrated to South Africa each year. Then, South Africa—with enough land for tens of millions of people—suddenly became too cramped, so they put a stop to immigration. But for the couple of weeks when people could still slip into that Garden of Eden, it is hard to convey what went on in small-town Jewish communities and emigration offices. It was like a large-scale fire broke out. Hundreds of telegrams flew from South Africa to Kovne and Warsaw, and from there to the towns, where hundreds of wives raced to join their husbands, and children their parents. One can say with certainty that the emigration offices rescued many people. They practically pulled boat tickets out of thin air. They often simply forced the consuls to give people visas. They also helped with money for boat tickets and the sums that immigrants were required to have on arrival. In short, they rescued and pushed through as many Jewish emigrants as they possibly could during those couple of weeks.

During this time, scenes played out that were reminiscent of the story of the wealthy Jewish woman during the Roman siege of Jerusalem. She sent a maidservant to buy white bread in the market, but the servant could not get white bread, so she returned to ask if she should take half-white, and then black bread and so forth, until she ended up with nothing.[2]

The price of boat tickets soared. Poor Jews traveled in first class because there were no tickets for third class; by the time a woman got enough money for second class, those tickets had already been snapped up, so she had to try to find the money for first class. The same thing happened with the quantity of money immigrants were required to possess on arrival. Both the emigrants and the emigration offices were in a feverish state. Nonetheless, they pushed through even more people than they had hoped.

---

2   {Leshchinsky refers here to the Talmudic story of Marta bat Baitos. In the original, the servant is male and he is sent successively for fine flour, ordinary flour, coarse flour, and barley flour. *Talmud Bavli*. C. 200–500 BCE. Gittin 56a: 11. https://www.sefaria.org/Gittin.13a.6?lang=bi.}

There stand before us two Jewish refugees from Russia who crossed the border illegally. I will spare the details of what crossing the Soviet-Polish border entails. It means being more dead than alive. They are lucky; they made it to the other side. Now they are ready to continue suffering as much as necessary, as long as they can make it to their relatives in Argentina. And that is where a series of tasks must be undertaken that, without an emigration bureau, would surely result in these Jews disappearing or getting deported back to Russia. The Polish authorities must be persuaded to allow them to remain until they depart for Argentina. Visas, boat tickets, and dozens of documents—every day a new one—must be obtained. These two Jews are practically mute, since they only know Yiddish and a little Russian. Every task is a mountain of hardships, hustling, requests, pleas, and telegrams to relatives in Argentina. With every task, two Jewish lives are literally being saved from ruin.

These are all typical cases. The two souls wandering far from home in need of rescue, the girl who has lost her parents, the couple of hundred emigrants trying to make it to South Africa before the country is closed to them—these are all everyday occurrences that can be observed in any emigration office.

It is sufficient to say that the Vilna emigration office, for example, has thus far been involved with emigrants destined for 35 countries. Jews travel to every corner of the world: Honduras, Peru, Chile, Venezuela, China, Japan, Guatemala, India, not to mention all the countries of Western Europe and the well-established destination countries, like America, Argentina, Brazil, Uruguay, and others. Simply providing information about obtaining a visa for all of these countries, with the various laws and obstacles faced upon arrival, is a task with immense social value.

No less important are the money transfers. A relative who sends his family members $100–200 directly and is not overly worried about what they will do with the money uses a private bank, rather than HIAS. But imagine a relative who is earning barely enough to live on in America. When he sends his poor relatives in Europe even $30–40, he is depriving his own children. A relative like this wants to take care of his family in Europe not with alms tossed their way, but with assistance that will get results: aid that will get them back on their own feet, or aid distributed in such a way that it will be sufficient for several months.

A Jew from a tiny town in Poland asks his relative for $50 to purchase a workshop or a small store, to build a roof for his house, to migrate to Brazil, to buy a cow as a source of income, or to provide a dowry for a daughter. Any private bank would disburse the $50 and would not go and check whether the workshop has been purchased, whether the house has been built and is just missing a roof, or whether there really is a groom for the old maid and the only thing missing is money for the dowry. The bank could not care less; it handed over the money, and the recipient can do with it whatever he pleases.

It happens very often that before the groom turns up, or before a store or workshop can be bought, the money has already been consumed, and the family again goes crying and begging for help and salvation from the American relative.

HIAS takes a very different approach to these situations. HIAS is not a bank with heartless, stiff-collared employees. It is a social bank with a heart and an understanding of the needs of both the givers and the recipients. If the rabbi does not have the engagement contract, it will not disburse the dowry; if there are no boat tickets, it will not disburse the money sent explicitly for emigration to Brazil or Argentina; if no workshop has been purchased, it will not disburse the aid meant solely for that purpose, and not for food. Here lies the great service, the major social accomplishment of money transfers via HIAS: someone can achieve a particular result for their relative. From New York, a specific goal can be set for money sent to Shnipishok or Kutne, and a faithful messenger ensures that this goal is reached.

This often leads to comical situations in small Jewish towns. It happens, for example, that a groom does not want to sign the engagement contract or refuses to go to the *khupe*[3] until he has the money in his pocket. The bride's father, on the other hand, is afraid to turn the money over. HIAS, which has been given the money for the purpose of the young woman's marriage, is also unwilling to disburse it before the wedding. HIAS, however, is seen as absolutely trustworthy and can be taken at its word. If HIAS tells the groom that after the wedding, he will receive the dowry, everyone heads happily to the *khupe* and dances with joy afterwards.

---

3   {A *khupe* is a canopy used for the marriage ceremony at traditional Jewish weddings.}

Thus, HIAS is not some disinterested bank official, but a messenger that brings couples together in marriage, and likewise (forgive the comparison) separates them in divorce. A husband has been in America for several years and has lost interest in his wife back home in a Polish town, so he does not want to bring her over. He wants to obtain a divorce so that he can remarry. She demands money and he agrees. However, he stipulates that the money should only be disbursed to her when she provides a Jewish and civil divorce. He is too skeptical to provide the money and she is too skeptical to provide the divorce. HIAS steps in and untangles this difficult knot. When HIAS tells the wife that the money is with them—not with that scoundrel who abandoned his poor wife to find his happiness with other women—and that they will disburse it after the divorce, everything is resolved.

When someone sends money to pay for an orphan's school tuition, would a private bank make sure to pay tuition every month? And when someone sends money for a Jewish woman's operation, with the condition that the money only be given to the surgical clinic, would a bank really ensure that she had the operation, rather than using the money for other expenses?

These are all individual tribulations of American relatives trying to help their families in Europe and ensure that their money really does bring about salvation. But here is another case to consider. A *landsmanshaft* sends money to a town to be distributed among the neediest.[4] For instance, the Zhirardov *landsmanshaft* sent 306 dollars for 32 people. What bank would take on this kind of responsibility? And if they sent the money by post, how much money would disappear or get sent back because the addresses were incorrect, the names did not match, or this or that impoverished person living in a hovel somewhere could not be located? HIAS sent two people from Warsaw to distribute the money among the needy people.

It is well known that we Jews have complicated names, and these become complicated even further by relatives in America. A man might be registered as "Motl" in his passport, but his relative writes "Mordkhe." A woman might be registered as "Taybl," but everybody calls her "Tanye," so her relative writes "Tanye." Someone might be registered

---

4 {A *landsmanshaft* is an association of Jews from the same Central or Eastern European village, town, or city.}

12. Emigration tragedies

Fig. 8 Poster (undated), Warsaw, Poland. ©Archives of the YIVO Institute for Jewish Research, New York. The poster asks: "Do you have relatives in America, Canada, Argentina, Cuba, Mexico, or other countries? Do you want to get in touch with them and receive money, affidavits, etc., from them? Then turn to your local committee that is in close contact with HIAS. Information free for everyone. The office is located at _____ and is open from _____ to _____." http://polishjews.yivoarchives.org/archive/index.php?p=digitallibrary/digitalcontent&id=863

as "Moyshe" but his American relative feels like writing "Moses." Of course, the post office refuses to deliver the money. A "real" bank, a bank that does not understand these Jewish notions, sends the money back to the relative in New York. A holiday is approaching. Moyshe is looking forward to a few dollars, while Taybl is sick and waiting on money from her sister. In both cases, however, the unfortunate misnomers get in the way. There is no money to be had, so they can say goodbye to the holiday celebrations and the trip to the doctor. HIAS, on the other hand, is not a real bank. It is a Jewish institution that *does* understand the tricks with Jewish names; it knows how "Dvoyre" becomes "Dory" and "Etl" becomes "Cleopatra." It has enough sense to ask the town's rabbi or doctor, and a few days later the money is disbursed.

How many tragedies are thus avoided? How many lives are saved? How many holidays are kept from ruin? And all because HIAS is not a real bank with ice-cold clerks who care only about the money, rather than giving a single thought to living people. HIAS also ensures that the money is delivered in full to the intended recipients. HIAS is a Jewish social institution that knows that real people are waiting with bated breath for a mail carrier to deliver the news that money has arrived from America.

In the current state of danger for Jews throughout Eastern Europe, rescuing several hundred or several thousand Jewish emigrants is a greater accomplishment than helping a hundred thousand Jewish migrants before the World War. Providing a poor widow, orphan, or entire family with $10 in a timely fashion is no smaller deed than sending $1,000 before the war. If one reflects on current emigration work, its value for emigrants, and the obstacles it faces, it is impossible to speak carelessly about the emigration institutions.

Index

Africa 132
agune 100
Ahad Ha'am xii
Aleichem, Sholem 48
Aleksandrov 123
Alexander 48
Alt, Volf 53
antisemitism, popular xi, xiii, xv, 18, 27, 88, 90, 100, 102–103, 118, 120, 126, 130, 134
antisemitism, state 65, 67, 102, 122, 124, 126, 129, 134
apprentices 68, 101, 129
Argentina xvi, 144–145, 147
artisans, artisanal work(ers) xiv, 62, 64–65, 67–68, 80, 88, 106–107, 111, 121, 129, 131
Asch, Sholem 3, 27
Asia 55
assimilation (ethnic, religious) xvi, 3–5, 13, 17, 19, 21–22, 25–29, 48, 89, 117, 135–136
Australia 132
Austria xiii, 17, 26
Austro-Hungarian Empire 8, 17, 122

Balkan countries 55
Baluty 114–117
banks xv, 15, 22, 45, 48, 55, 62–63, 72, 75, 95, 105, 127, 144–147
Belarus xiii, 6, 62
Berezovka 52
Berlin xii, 59, 104
Bern xii
Bialystok 5, 7–8, 11, 13, 33–34, 36–37, 39, 46, 51–52, 54–55, 72, 97, 132–133
Bolshevik Jewish policy 61, 69, 71
Bramson, Leon 18
Brazil 132, 144–145

Brest 7
Bundism 36, 66, 120, 124, 130
Byala 67, 123

Canada xvi, 147
Carpathia 3, 6
Caucasus 79
Central America 132
cheder, cheders (pl.) 6, 17, 34–35, 37, 46, 49, 53
Chicago 59
Chile 144
China 55, 144
Cohen, Asher 48–49
cohesion, social 20
communism xi, xv, 36, 60, 85, 90, 135
cottage work(ers), home work(ers) 18, 31, 33
Cuba 147
Czechoslovakia xiii
Czestochowa 5, 52, 82

Diamand, Herman 17
diasporism xii, xv
Drobnin 51

Eitingon, Boris 49–50
Eitingon, Mikhoel 49
Eitingon, Naum 49–50
elul 135–136
emigration xi, xv, 34, 73, 80, 131–132, 141–145, 148
England 9, 55
English (language) xix, 100
Europe xv–xvi, 2, 6, 25, 27, 34, 60, 66, 144, 146, 148

factory owners, entrepreneurs 13, 16, 34–35, 38–43, 45–48, 51–55, 60–62, 65, 72–73, 75–76, 103–105, 109, 128–129

Jewish 14, 43, 46, 53, 61, 73, 129
non-Jewish 45
factory work(ers) xiv, 6–7, 9, 12–16, 18,
  23–24, 33–35, 37, 39–43, 45–51, 53–55,
  61–64, 66–67, 72, 78, 80, 87–88, 90–91,
  102–104, 107–108, 110, 113–115,
  117–124, 126, 129, 131
  Jewish xiv, 14–15, 33, 35, 41–43, 45–46,
    51, 54, 61, 63, 67, 72, 80, 90, 103–104,
    113, 115, 117, 119–121, 124, 129
  non-Jewish 7, 14, 33, 39–41, 45
fairs 9, 97
Far East 55
Forverts xii, 90
Foyst, Herman 52

Gabin 53
Galicia 3–4, 6, 9–10, 17, 63, 92, 122, 133
gemora 21, 35–37, 42, 48–49, 53
geographical segregation 3–4
Germany xii–xiii, xv, 3, 9, 26, 39–40, 45,
  49, 51–52, 54–56, 72, 128, 142
gmiles khsodim 131
Goebbels, Joseph 137
grain industry 10, 35, 60, 64–66, 73–74,
  106, 122
Grodno 6–7, 10, 39, 61, 87, 123
Guatemala 144

hasid, hasidim (pl.), hasidism xvi, 16,
  49–50, 52, 118, 125, 135–136
haskala, Jewish enlightenment 49, 135
Hebrew xix, 6, 27–28, 36, 98, 142
Heinzel, Julius 52
Herts, Moyshe 48
Herzl, Theodor 35
HIAS, Hebrew Immigrant Aid Society
  142, 144–148
Hitler, Adolf 137
Honduras 144
Horodyshche xii
Hrubeshov 123
Hungary 6, 55

India 144
inflation 55, 77, 104, 106, 126, 128

institutional autonomy 19–21
Israel xiii, xix, 1, 36–37, 127

Japan 55, 144
Joint Distribution Committee, Joint 60,
  117, 131

kahal, kehila, kehilot (pl.) 19, 21
Kahan, Lazar 46, 51
  *Ilustrirter yorbukh far industri, handl
  un finansn* 46
Kahan, Yankev 52–53
kapore 135
Katowice 49, 51
Khelm 123
Kherson 79
khupe 145
Kielce xi, 8
Kiev xii, 71, 136
Konin 123
Kotzk 50
Kovel 53
Kovno 133
Krakow 5, 8, 21, 52, 82, 133, 136
Kutne 136, 145

Labour Zionism xii
landowners 11, 31, 45, 47, 62, 64, 68,
  90–91, 122
landsmanshaft 146
Latvia 66, 141
Leipzig 9
Lemberg 8, 82–84, 89–91, 97, 107–109,
  130, 132–133, 136. *See also* Lvov
Leshchinsky, Yankev xii–xvi, xix, 4, 10,
  95, 108–109, 114, 143
liberalism xvi, 17, 22, 49
Lieberman, Hermann 17
Lipno 123
Lipshitz, Yerakhmiel 50–51
liquor concessions 51, 63–64
Lithuania 3, 6–7, 11, 35, 66, 74, 79, 141
Lodz 5, 8, 13, 16, 28, 39–42, 46, 48–53,
  73–74, 83, 103, 109, 113–114, 116–121,
  127–128, 130, 133, 136, 138–139
London 89, 114

loynketnik 35, 37
Lublin 5, 8, 19, 21, 53, 67, 82, 123
lumber industry (forestry) 63–66, 105–106, 129
Lvov 5, 8, 82, 98, 100. *See also* Lemberg

markets, urban 4, 18, 22–23, 34, 55–56, 64, 66, 72–74, 80, 95, 97–102, 115, 119, 121, 133–134, 137, 143
Medem, Vladimir 35
Meir Bal-Nes, Rabbi 37
Mendele Moykher Sforim 106
Mexico 35, 38, 147
Mikhalovo 52
Minsk 7, 10, 79, 92, 133
Mishtsanov 123
misnagdic (anti-Hasidic) 125
Mlawa 12
Moscow 49, 77, 97
Moss, Kenneth B. xvi, xix

Naselsk 123
National Bolshevik Jewish policy 61–62, 65, 69
Navidvar 123
New York xii, 38, 59, 132, 145, 147
Nomberg, Hersh 27
Novogrodek 8, 51

Odessa xii, 46, 52
oil industry 63, 88
Opatoshu, Yosef 27
Orsha 49
ORT, Association for the Promotion of Skilled Trades 60, 117, 120
Ostrovets 123
Otvotsk 87, 103
Ozorkow 50

Pabianice 49, 52
Palestine xv–xvi, 60, 127
Peretz, Y. L. 27, 37, 97
 A Night in the Old Market 97
Perl, Felix 17
Peru 144
Petrikov 51

peyes 88, 114, 135–136
Pikelni, Avrom 51
Pinsk 7, 62–63, 65, 105–106
Plotsk 51
pogrom 20, 39, 71, 82–83, 90–92, 95, 125–127
Poland xi, xiii–xvii, 1–29, 32–33, 35, 42, 45, 50, 52, 55, 59–63, 65–69, 71–76, 79–80, 82–93, 95, 97–98, 102–104, 108–110, 116, 118–120, 122–123, 125–131, 133–136, 138, 141, 144–147
Poleskie 8
political segregation 1, 5, 14–18, 22, 27–28
Pomerania 10–11
population density 3–4, 19
Poretski and Govenski 51
Posen 10–11, 24, 26, 127–128, 133
Poznanski, Israel 48
Poznanski, Kalman 48
proletarianization xiv
promissory note 41, 55–56, 71–75, 77–78, 95, 128, 131
Prusak, Avrom Moyshe 51–52
Przedbórz 49

Radom 133
rebbe 52, 118
residential segregation 3–6, 12–13, 15–17
Romania 6, 36, 55, 141
Rosenblat, Y. 49
Rovne 86–87, 123
Rubin, Zalmen 48
Russia xi–xiii, 1, 3–4, 6–10, 12, 17–19, 22, 24, 26, 35, 38–39, 45, 55, 59–60, 62, 65–66, 69, 71, 73, 78–80, 90–93, 96, 119, 122, 127, 133, 135, 141–142, 144

salt industry 60, 62, 64, 88
Segalovitch, Zusman 27
Shedlets 142
Sheps, Y. 53
Shtutshin 51
Shulzinger, Fayvl 50
Sienkiewicz, Henryk 35
Silesia 10, 133

Singer, Isaac Bashevis 27
Slonim 123
Slovakia 6
socialism xii, xv–xvi, 15, 17–18, 35, 42, 90, 104, 116, 120, 135–136
socio-economic segregation 8–17
Sosnowiec 5
South Africa 143–144
South America 132
Stanislav 8
state employment, civil servants 10, 66, 122, 129
state nationalization 23, 29, 60, 65, 129
storekeepers 6, 12–13, 15–16, 18, 23, 25, 31, 34, 46–48, 62, 64, 67, 73–76, 80, 99, 107, 125, 127, 130–131
suicide 84–85, 105, 121, 130–131, 136
sweating system 33
Switzerland xii

Talmud 6, 21, 36, 49, 125, 143
Tarnopol 8
taxation, taxes xiv, 13, 16, 63, 67–69, 87–88, 95, 98–99, 102, 107, 109, 111, 126, 128, 130–131, 134
tefillin 35, 135
territorialism 20
textile industry xiv, 8–10, 13, 24, 33–34, 40, 45–51, 54–55, 72–73, 77, 104–106, 118, 121, 127–128, 130
Teytelboym brothers 53
tobacco industry 22, 34, 60–62, 64, 87–88
Tomashev 49, 53
Tomaszów 51
Tsitron, Sh. H. 52
tsitses 114

Ukraine xii–xiii, 3–4, 7–8, 11–12, 24, 26, 79, 90, 92–93, 135

United States of America xii–xiii, xvi, 1, 27–28, 34, 40, 51, 59–60, 73, 108, 125, 132, 141–148
Uruguay 144
U.S.S.R. xiii, 1, 66, 69

Vasilishki 51
Venezuela 144
Vilna xii, 5, 7–8, 13, 51, 74, 82–83, 85, 92, 97, 107–109, 125–134, 144
Vinaver, Maksim Moiseevich 18
Vistula River 2–3, 138
Vitebsk 133
Vladimir-Volynsk 123
Vlotzlavek 136
Volhynia 8, 11, 92

Warsaw xii, xiv, 5, 8, 13–14, 16, 23, 28, 46, 48, 53, 61, 66–68, 71, 78–79, 81–85, 91, 96–97, 103–105, 109, 118–121, 123–124, 128, 130, 132–133, 136–138, 143, 146–147
Washington 67
Wilkoszewski, Bronisław 50
Wittlin, Józef 27
World War I xiii, 1, 4, 7–8, 20, 133, 142, 148
World War II xi, 96

yeshiva, yeshivas (pl.) 6, 17, 20–21, 35, 37, 46, 51–53, 110, 135–136
Yiddish (language) xii–xiii, xix, 4–6, 27–28, 35–37, 68, 79, 135, 141, 144
Yugoslavia 55

Zdunska Wola 51
Zhirardov 146
Zilbershteyn, Markus 49
Zionism xii, xv, 35–36, 118, 127

About the Team

Alessandra Tosi was the managing editor for this book.

Mihaela Buna and Alessandra Tosi proofread the manuscript.

Melissa Purkiss indexed the book.

Jeevanjot Kaur Nagpal designed the cover. The cover was produced in InDesign using the Fontin font.

Luca Baffa typeset the book in InDesign and produced the paperback and hardback editions. The text font is Tex Gyre Pagella; the heading font is Californian FB.

Luca produced the EPUB, AZW3, PDF and HTML editions — the conversion is performed with open source software such as pandoc (https://pandoc.org/) created by John MacFarlane and other tools freely available on our GitHub page (https://github.com/OpenBookPublishers).

Sacha PG-Tanna produced the XML edition.

This book need not end here...

Share

All our books — including the one you have just read — are free to access online so that students, researchers and members of the public who can't afford a printed edition will have access to the same ideas. This title will be accessed online by hundreds of readers each month across the globe: why not share the link so that someone you know is one of them?

This book and additional content is available at:

https://doi.org/10.11647/OBP.0341

Donate

Open Book Publishers is an award-winning, scholar-led, not-for-profit press making knowledge freely available one book at a time. We don't charge authors to publish with us: instead, our work is supported by our library members and by donations from people who believe that research shouldn't be locked behind paywalls.

Why not join them in freeing knowledge by supporting us: https://www.openbookpublishers.com/support-us

Follow @OpenBookPublish

Read more at the Open Book Publishers **BLOG**

You may also be interested in:

The Pogroms in Ukraine, 1918–19
Prelude to the Holocaust
Maurice Wolfthal

https://doi.org/10.11647/OBP.0176

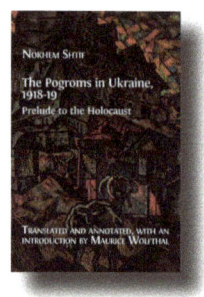

Photography in the Third Reich
Art, Physiognomy and Propaganda
Christopher Webster

https://doi.org/10.11647/OBP.0202

Brownshirt Princess
A Study of the 'Nazi Conscience'
Lionel Gossman

https://doi.org/10.11647/OBP.0003

www.ingramcontent.com/pod-product-compliance
Lightning Source LLC
Chambersburg PA
CBHW041313240426
43669CB00024B/2977